Soccer

Other titles in the Science Behind Sports series:

SCIENCE BEHIND SPORTS

Soccer

JENNY MACKAY

LUCENT BOOKS

A part of Gale, Cengage Learning

GALE
CENGAGE Learning™

Detroit • New York • San Francisco • New Haven, Conn • Waterville, Maine • London

LIBRARY OF CONGRESS CATALOGING-IN-PUBLICATION DATA

MacKay, Jenny, 1978-
  Soccer / by Jenny MacKay.
    p. cm. — (Science behind sports)
  Includes bibliographical references and index.
  ISBN 978-1-4205-0572-6 (hardcover)
1. Soccer. 2. Sports sciences. I. Title.
  GV943.M318 2011
  796.334—dc22
                                                    2011003419

Lucent Books
27500 Drake Rd
Farmington Hills MI 48331

ISBN-13: 978-1-4205-0572-6
ISBN-10: 1-4205-0572-6

Printed in the United States of America
1 2 3 4 5 6 7 15 14 13 12 11

Printed by Bang Printing, Brainerd, MN, 1st Ptg., 05/2011

TABLE OF CONTENTS

FOREWORD

On March 21, 1970, Slovenian ski jumper Vinko Bogataj took a terrible fall while competing at the Ski-flying World Championships in Oberstdorf, West Germany. Bogataj's pinwheeling crash was caught on tape by an ABC *Wide World of Sports* film crew and eventually became synonymous with "the agony of defeat" in competitive sporting. While many viewers were transfixed by the severity of Bogataj's accident, most were not aware of the biomechanical and environmental elements behind the skier's fall—heavy snow and wind conditions that made the ramp too fast and Bogataj's inability to maintain his center of gravity and slow himself down. Bogataj's accident illustrates that, no matter how mentally and physically prepared an athlete may be, scientific principles—such as momentum, gravity, friction, and aerodynamics—always have an impact on performance.

Lucent Books' Science Behind Sports series explores these and many more scientific principles behind some of the most popular team and individual sports, including baseball, hockey, gymnastics, wrestling, swimming, and skiing. Each volume in the series focuses on one sport or group of related sports. The volumes open with a brief look at the featured sport's origins, history and changes, then move on to cover the biomechanics and physiology of playing, related health and medical concerns, and the causes and treatment of sports-related injuries.

In addition to learning about the arc behind a curve ball, the impact of centripetal force on a figure skater, or how water buoyancy helps swimmers, Science Behind Sports readers will also learn how exercise, training, warming up, and diet and nutrition directly relate to peak performance and enjoyment of the sport. Volumes may also cover why certain sports are popular, how sports function in the business world, and which hot sporting issues—sports doping and cheating, for example—are in the news.

Basic physical science concepts, such as acceleration, kinetics, torque, and velocity, are explained in an engaging and accessible manner. The full-color text is augmented by fact boxes, sidebars, photos, and detailed diagrams, charts and graphs. In addition, a subject-specific glossary, bibliography and index provide further tools for researching the sports and concepts discussed throughout Science Behind Sports.

CHAPTER 1

The People's Game

Soccer—or as it is known throughout most of the world, football—is the most popular sport on Earth, and the roots of the game may be as old as the human race itself. From the time children can walk, they are able to kick small objects with their feet. There is something irresistible about the ability to send a pebble flying in a new direction with a strike of the toes, and the earliest humans, just like humans today, did that from time to time. They eventually kicked larger objects, such as fruits and gourds. More than one person might have joined in the fun, turning a mere kicking session into something with a purpose: passing the object to another person or keeping it away from someone else. Rules were made about the type of object to be kicked and how to determine a winner. At that point, the mere act of kicking an object transformed into a game with guidelines, winners, and losers. In the most general sense, it was a sport.

The modern game of soccer—called football almost everywhere but in the United States, Canada, and New Zealand—is widely believed to have its ball-kicking origins in ancient human experiences. Historians believe that kicking games started not in just one place but in different cultures and on different continents of the globe. "Football is as old as the world," says Sepp Blatter, president of the

Fédération Internationale de Football Association (FIFA), the international governing body of professional soccer. "People have always played some form of football, from its very basic form of kicking a ball around to the game it is today."[1] Throughout history, kicking games and human culture often have developed side by side.

Soccer in Ancient Asia

Some of the earliest records of a kicking game played for sport come from China. About 200 B.C., the Chinese invented a kickball-style sport that used a round ball made of leather and stuffed with silk, fur, or feathers. Players were divided into two teams, and the game was played on an area with marked edges to define the boundaries. There was a

Japanese priests and monks dressed in traditional costumes play kemari, an ancient ball-kicking game that is still played in Japan today.

goal in the middle of the playing area, a silk sheet pulled taut between two bamboo poles. The sheet had a hole about 12 inches (30cm) wide for the ball to pass through so a team could score. Like the modern sport of soccer, players in this early Chinese ball game were able to use any body part except their hands. Unlike the modern game, however, the goals were positioned about 30 feet (9m) above the ground. It required great strength and skill to pass the heavy leather ball through the hole in the sheet without using hands. The sport was called *cuju* or *t'su chu*.

Several centuries after the first records were made of *cuju*, the Japanese created their own form of ball-kicking game called *kemari*, which used a deerskin ball 9 to 10 inches (23cm to 25cm) in diameter and stuffed with sawdust. Players set out to keep the ball from touching the ground by juggling it—keeping it in the air and passing it to other players using their feet, knees, and chests but not their hands. *Kemari* teams consisted of eight men, and they played within the boundaries of a rectangular field marked by specific trees in each corner—cherry, maple, willow, and pine. The sport did not pit one team against another; rather, everyone on the field worked together with the common objective of keeping the ball from touching the ground. Once a certain number of consecutive "juggles" had been accomplished, which could be up to one thousand, the game was over. *Kemari*'s heyday in Japan ended by the sixteenth century A.D., but some Japanese still play it.

Ball-kicking games in ancient China and Japan were more than just ways for people to kill time. The games also had cultural importance. *Kemari* was sometimes played as part of Japanese ceremonies to ward off misfortune. *Cuju* was sometimes used as a form of military training and also was linked to traditional Chinese ideas and ways of thought. According to classical history professor Nigel B. Crowther, "ancient handbooks (including one of the earliest surviving Chinese texts) show how important *cuju* grew to be in Chinese society."[2] He says the game was even seen to represent traditional, spiritual Chinese ideas, such as the opposite concepts of yin and yang and that the ball represented one of the heavenly bodies. Games like *cuju* were very symbolic in

Bouncing Back

The concept of rubber balls came to soccer from native South Americans, who discovered that the sap from their native gum tree was bouncy. Rubber was fascinating, but it had its limitations, too—it melted in hot weather and became brittle when temperatures were cold. An American inventor named Charles Goodyear was determined to find a way to make rubber weatherproof and temperature resistant, and in 1836 he found the answer. A process of treating rubber with sulphur and then heating it made it retain its shape and properties in all weather conditions. Vulcanized rubber, named after Vulcan, the Roman god of fire, was born. In 1855 Goodyear created the first soccer ball out of vulcanized rubber. The ball's panels resembled those of modern-day basketballs. It was used in a soccer match in Boston in 1863 and became the trophy for the game. That trophy ball of vulcanized rubber was donated to the Society for the Preservation of New England Antiquities in 1925.

ancient cultures because they mirrored the values and ideas that people believed in. The field was a symbol of the earth, for example, the ball symbolized the sun, and the players symbolized mankind living and playing on Earth under the sun. Playing or watching a game like *cuju* may have been an important way for many ancient people to show their faith and belief in spiritual ideas like heaven and Earth.

Kicking Games in the Americas

China and Japan were not the only cultures of the ancient world in which kickball games were important features of daily life. Similar games developed on other continents and also reflected their culture's religious and philosophical beliefs. Some of the people of ancient South and Central America had an especially strong spiritual connection to kicking games, which may have even older origins than games played by ancient cultures in Asia. The long history of

Among the sites at the ruins of Chichén Itzá in Mexico is the Great Ballcourt, a walled field where ball-kicking games were played by the Mayan people.

ball games in the Americas has been demonstrated in Paso de la Amada in Mexico, where modern archaeological digs have turned up a ball field that is estimated to be thirty-five hundred years old. In the modern-day countries of Mexico, Guatemala, Belize, and Honduras, ball-kicking sports are believed to have been popular for three thousand years and were probably played by every society in Central America. "Over 1,500 ball courts have been unearthed," says soccer historian and author David Goldblatt. "The sheer number of courts and ubiquity of objects indicated that the game was played informally by commoners as well as ritually by the elite."[3] The ancient Mayas, who lived in the rain forests of Mexico and Guatemala from about A.D. 300 to 900, also placed extreme importance on kicking games, so much so that their beliefs about the very creation of their culture were rooted in a ball game in which two twin brothers defeated the gods and later became the sun and moon in the sky. It was not uncommon for players of Mayan ball games to be sacrificed to the gods at the end of a match.

Ball games were so important in Mayan culture that their playing fields had phenomenal proportions. One of the world's most famous ancient landmarks is the Great Ball Court at the Mayan ruins of Chichén Itzá, an archaeological site in modern-day Mexico's Yucatán Peninsula. The ball court is 545 feet (166m) long and 225 feet (69m) wide, almost twice the size of a modern soccer field. It has a temple-like structure at either end, perhaps where ancient royalty gathered to watch important games. Despite the field's enormous size and the fact that it is open to the sky, a human whispering at one end of the court can be heard clearly by someone standing at the other end. The acoustics (physical properties that relate to sound) of the Great Ball Court remain a mystery, but the 23-foot-tall (7m) parallel walls along the length of the field are believed to create a "flutter echo" effect in which sound waves bounce from wall to wall to carry sounds up or down the court. The Mayans' attention to every small detail of the Great Ball Court, even its acoustics, shows the importance that ball-kicking games had in that culture and, historians believe, in nearly every other culture of Central America leading up to European colonization in the 1400s and 1500s. "In some Latin American areas soccer is simply called *pelota* (ball)—as if the only ball game existing or imaginable is soccer," says Richard Witzig, a physician who has worked with the World Health Organization and has played semiprofessional soccer. "This illustrates the central cultural position soccer occupies in Latin American countries."[4]

Ball-kicking games were not just popular among ancient Mayans and other cultures of Central America. When the first English colonists arrived on the North American coast in what is now the state of Massachusetts in 1620, they

CROWDED OUT

24.3 million
Number of Americans who watched either a television or Internet broadcast of the 2010 World Cup finals game in South Africa, making it the most-watched soccer game in U.S. history.

wrote about Native Americans playing a ball game called *pasuckquakkohwog*, or "they gather to play ball with the foot." And when the Spanish colonized Central and South America, they discovered something even more unique about American ball games than their widespread popularity across two continents—many American balls bounced, because they were made from the sap of rubber trees native to Central America. Ball games played with rubber balls were far different than those played with the heavy, feather-stuffed leather variety used elsewhere in the world. Europeans took the rubber balls back home to change the experience of ball playing on a continent that had inherited its own versions of ball games from the ancient Romans and Greeks.

Ball Play in Europe

Europeans, too, played various forms of ball games by the 1700s and 1800s, borrowing elements from the ancient Greek game of *episkyros* and the ancient Roman game

Members of a soccer team from London's Addiscombe Military College pose together in 1855. As the popularity of the sport spread throughout England in the 1800s, many boys' schools began fielding teams to compete with other schools.

of *harpastum*. In *episkyros*, teams of young Greek men battled on a field to throw and kick a ball over a central line while trying to force the opposing team over its rear boundary line and thus win the game. *Episkyros* was probably used as much for military training as for a pastime. The ancient Roman game of *harpastum* was a lot like the modern-day children's game of keep-away or monkey-in-the-middle, the object being to throw and kick the ball away from someone else. Games similar to *episkyros* and *harpastum* were still played around Europe in the nineteenth century. The new rubber balls and ball-playing techniques brought back to Europe from colonies in the New World, however, helped renew European and especially English interest in ball games and ultimately changed the history of sports worldwide.

In English society, sports had always been sharply divided along class lines between rich and poor. Favorite sports of the wealthy, such as hunting and polo played on horseback, differed from the favorite sports of the underclass, such as ball-kicking games that required nothing but a ball and two teams willing to play. By the 1700s and 1800s, ball games among the poorer classes had evolved into wildly popular and often violent matches. Entire neighboring towns sometimes battled against one another in the struggle to move the ball across the other team's goal. English ball games were officially banned by various kings at different times in history, because they were believed to threaten public safety and social order. But then a new tradition came about in English society—boys' schools, where upper-class young men went to live and to learn. With the creation and spread of English schools, boys who had few ways to spend free time took up ball games. Schools formed teams and competed against other schools. These teams quickly learned that they could not play fairly against each other without a standard set of rules, so they formed ball game

WHAT'S IN A NAME?

soccer

The word first used by the British as an abbreviation of "association football," or football without hands, as opposed to *rugger*, or rugby-style football.

regulations. The groundwork of modern-day soccer as an international, organized sport was laid in the mid-1800s in the boys' schools of England.

The First Soccer Rules

Early football games at some English schools allowed hands to be used during play, while at other schools the use of hands was forbidden. As the schoolboys grew up, they took their favorite games with them to college. The debate over whether hands should be used in college ball games became heated, with different schools taking different sides on the matter. In 1863, the first official football organization, the London Football Association, was formed in England. The members of this association wrote a set of official national rules to govern the game of football, including how many players could be on a team, how goals were to be scored, the dimensions of the playing

The Freemason's Tavern was the site where the London Football Association was formed in 1863. The association established the game's first official set of rules.

King of Soccer

Edson Arantes do Nascimento was born in 1940 in Brazil. He was nicknamed Pelé when he was just a kid, and he played soccer in the dirt streets of his Brazilian hometown. Pelé is now the world's most spectacular soccer star. Pelé was chosen for Brazil's national team when he was fifteen years old, and he played in his first World Cup in 1958 at age seventeen. He became the youngest scorer in FIFA World Cup history that year. Pelé later led Brazil to three World Cup titles in 1958, 1962, and 1970. During his twenty-two-year career, Pelé scored a total of 1,281 goals. He excelled at every aspect of the game, dribbling the ball around competitors with split-second fake outs and bouncing it off his own feet to trick opponents. He was notorious for lobbing the ball over competitors' heads only to retrieve it on the other side for a score. His fancy tricks dismayed goalkeepers and delighted fans. Named the FIFA Player of the Century, Pelé is a sports legend the world over. He called soccer *o jogo bonito*, "the beautiful game," and no player has ever made it look as good as Pelé.

Brazilian soccer star Pelé (right) shoots the ball in his team's victorious World Cup final game in 1958. He also led Brazil to World Cup titles in 1962 and 1970 and became an international sports star.

field, and what players could and could not do during play. The most controversial rule was the no-hands rule, forbidding the use of hands to touch the ball or to hold or grab other players during a game. Players who preferred the hands-on version of football started their own sport, rugby. But it was football that secured the top place in the hearts of the people of England, then Europe, then the world. And it was football that became a worldwide phenomenon during the decades following that first official set of rules in 1863, rules that remain much the same in soccer today.

A Sport's Rise to Fame

Although many variations of ball-kicking games had existed for several millennia, the "new" English football changed the world. Born during the Industrial Revolution, a period of new technology, factories, and mass production of objects, the sport of soccer was positioned to enjoy a kind of success the human race had never before experienced in a pastime. For one thing, there was print media by then in the form of newspapers and telegrams, and these were efficient ways to inform people about official rules of the new sport and also to report on the outcomes of games. People in many different areas began to read about new teams and official matches in newspapers, and these people became the first sports fans. The Industrial Revolution also brought new transportation to Europe in the form of trains, which made it realistic for soccer teams to travel for games. This became increasingly important as England's fellow European countries put together their own

Teams from Bury and Southampton vie for the Football Association Cup championship before a large crowd at the Crystal Palace in London in 1900.

soccer teams. Whenever there was a game to watch, local spectators flocked to the soccer field. Entire towns and cities rallied around their team on game day and squeezed in for a space in another new phenomenon—the sports stadium, built to house soccer matches and the fans who turned out in droves to watch.

Seeing an opportunity for profit, organizers of soccer teams began charging admission for spectators to see a game. The Industrial Revolution was an era of paid factory and office jobs, and many workers in England and across Europe had a little money to spend. More and more, they spent it to watch soccer games. So powerful was the love of this new sport that it even changed the length of the average workweek. Since most soccer matches took place on Saturday, it became customary for employers to give their workers Saturday afternoon off in order to watch games. Before that, Saturday had been a full workday.

As soccer brought about changes to European society, the feverish love of the world's first officially organized sport traveled across continents and oceans to reach into nearly every corner of the world. Central and South American cultures took naturally to the sport, which was not dissimilar from kicking games they had been playing for thousands of years. Even small countries, such as the Caribbean island nation of Trinidad and Tobago, have taken up soccer in modern times, learned its official rules, and organized professional teams. In terms of its overall population, Trinidad and Tobago is the smallest nation ever represented in the World Cup, the international soccer tournament that takes place every four years. The participation of such a small country in the international soccer scene shows how influential the sport is around the world.

Soccer Today

Since its formalization in 1872, soccer has become the most-played and the most-watched sport on the planet. More of the world's nations and territories currently belong to FIFA than to the United Nations, the international organization dedicated to peace and improved standards

A GROWING OBSESSION

The final game of the 2010 FIFA World Cup was one of the most watched sporting events in history, with an estimated 600 million viewers. In the Netherlands alone, over fifty percent of the country's total population watched as their team lost to Spain, 0-1 in extra time.

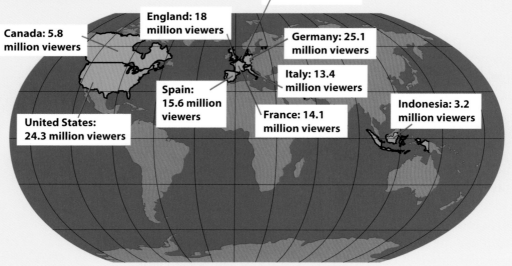

Netherlands: 8.5 million viewers

England: 18 million viewers

Canada: 5.8 million viewers

Germany: 25.1 million viewers

Italy: 13.4 million viewers

Spain: 15.6 million viewers

France: 14.1 million viewers

Indonesia: 3.2 million viewers

United States: 24.3 million viewers

of living worldwide. About 1.5 billion people watch one or more soccer games during a World Cup tournament. Due to television and the Internet, approximately 600 million people around the world, 1 in every 10 human beings, watched the World Cup finals in 2010. "It's the moment when the planet becomes a family, when we're all doing the same thing whether we are in California or Nigeria or Shanghai,"[5] says British sports journalist and author Simon Kuper.

One explanation for soccer's overwhelming worldwide popularity is that the sport is accessible to everyone. Soccer requires almost no specialized equipment—it can be played nearly anywhere there is a ball, from rural farms to urban streets. Almost anyone can learn to play soccer, too, whether they are male or female, large or small, muscular

or graceful, old or young. This is likely an important reason why the game is popular around the world, in wealthy countries as well as in poor ones. Soccer stars can come from anywhere and from any walk of life. It is "almost as if the human collective consciousness willed the game of soccer into being,"[6] says Witzig. Soccer is often referred to simply as the people's game.

Schoolgirls in Kenya play a game of soccer, which has become the world's most played and most watched sport, enjoyed by almost every culture.

CHAPTER 2

Goal Setting: The Physics of a Soccer Match

The people's game, accessible to almost anyone any-where, requires little more than a flat surface to use as a field and a ball to kick around. When playing in competition with others, however, the size of a soccer field, the shape and weight of the ball, and many other factors become important. Soccer, like any sport, is ruled by the laws of physics, or the science of objects in motion. The physical properties of the playing field, the movement of players on and within it, and the properties of the ball all become critical to how a particular soccer match is played and what its outcome will be. Every moment of the game depends on physics to determine how, whether, and when the ball will move across the field. In professional competitive play, much care is taken to make sure that the skill of the players, not characteristics of the ball or the playing field, controls who wins.

Size Matters

Soccer requires a standard set of regulations so that everyone plays by the same rules and opponents have an equal chance of winning. One thing official rules specify is the size of

An illustration of a soccer field shows the lines that indicate the overall perimeter, goal box, penalty area, and center line. The location of these lines and the rules they support, as well as the overall size of the field, are carefully configured to the physics of the game.

the rectangular soccer pitch, or playing field. The perimeter, the outer edge of the field, is marked with white lines. There is a goal box at the center point of each short end of the field, with a penalty area marked in front of the goal box. A centerline is also marked across the exact middle of the field. Many soccer rules depend on these lines, such as whether the ball can remain in play or has gone out of bounds and where players can stand at the start of a game. A typical soccer field for adult players is about 75 yards (69m) wide by 120 yards (110m) long, slightly larger than the size of a football field.

In a competitive soccer match, two teams of eleven players each face off. One player on each team is the goalkeeper, who attempts to keep the ball out of the goal and prevent the other team from scoring. With a total of twenty-two players moving on the field at one time, the field's dimensions are extremely important. "There must be a general relation between the number of players and the best size of the pitch," says physicist John Wesson. He continues,

> The essential factor is that there be pressure on the players to quickly control the ball and decide what to do with it. This means that opposing players must typically be able to run to the player with the ball in

a time comparable with the time taken to receive, control, and move the ball. If the distance between players is larger, the game loses tension. If the distance is much less the game has the appearance of a pinball machine.[7]

The size of an official soccer field and the number of players per team were not chosen at random. A field's dimensions give both teams a fair chance at stealing the ball from each other and at passing it effectively among their teammates. The field's size helps determine how players position themselves within it. They must gauge how fast the ball can travel, for example, and what trajectory or path the ball will take—whether it will rise over the heads of players or drop quickly to the ground. These details, governed by physics, determine whether and how fast a soccer ball will reach its intended recipient during a pass without rolling out of bounds.

The Almost Impossible Goal

In 1998, Roberto Carlos of the Spanish soccer team Real Madrid scored one of history's most inconceivable goals against rival team Tenerife. The ball was about to bounce out-of-bounds at the corner parallel to Tenerife's goal box. Carlos followed the ball at a full run and gave it a hard kick from a position nearly dead even with the goal post. Incredibly, the ball sailed just in front of the goal and curved left at the last moment to sink into the corner of the net.

Shots on goal have a triangular nature, with the corners of the goal box forming two points and the player kicking the ball forming the third point somewhere in front of the goal. In this case, Carlos's position skewed the triangle so far left of the goal as to be nearly a straight line. Carlos had to kick the ball across his body, hitting the inside of the ball with the outside of his left foot to give it enough spin to curve into the goal at the last second. The unlikely play stunned spectators, and video footage of the kick has enchanted physics enthusiasts ever since.

Friction, Gravity, and Newton's Laws

Resting objects, such as soccer balls, stay still if no force acts on them, and whenever a certain amount of force is applied to a resting object, it moves with predictable force. These phenomena were first described in the late 1600s by an English physicist named Isaac Newton, who described the behavior of any moving object with three simple statements, now known as Newton's laws of motion. Newton's first law of motion states that a moving object will stay in motion at the same speed, in a straight line, until another force (source of energy) acts on it to change its direction or rate of motion. His second law states that there is a relationship between the mass of an object and the amount of force that must be applied in order to move it at a specific velocity, or rate of motion. The third law of motion states that for every action, such as kicking a soccer ball, there is an equal and opposite reaction.

Newton's three laws are some of the most important facts in physics (and soccer games). Knowing that the rate or speed at which a resting object will move depends on the force applied to it, soccer players plan the force of their kicks to control the ball, keep it away from the other team, and move toward the other team's goal. They use knowledge of physics—what the ball will do once it is in motion—to position themselves close enough to or far enough from their teammates and opponents to have the best chance of completing, receiving, and intercepting passes. They also understand that any action, such as intercepting a ball, will cause an opposite reaction—a ball that hits a solid surface will naturally bounce the other way.

According to Newton's first law of motion, a resting soccer ball will not move until someone kicks it, and the direction and strength of the kick are essential. If a kick is too hard, the ball will sail over the players' heads and out of the field. If a kick is too soft, it will move slowly, giving the other team an opportunity to dash in and steal it. Skilled soccer players have learned to kick with just the right amount of force. They must use their muscles and body to harness a certain amount of energy, which is then passed to a soccer ball during a kick to set it in motion.

THE MAGNUS EFFECT

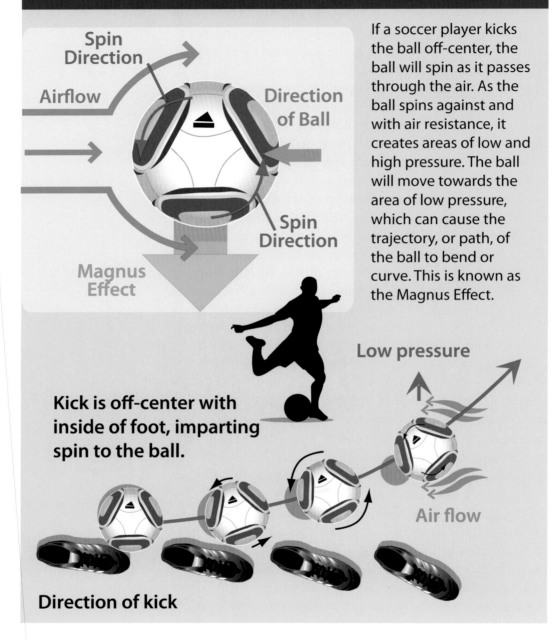

Spin Direction

Airflow

Direction of Ball

Spin Direction

Magnus Effect

If a soccer player kicks the ball off-center, the ball will spin as it passes through the air. As the ball spins against and with air resistance, it creates areas of low and high pressure. The ball will move towards the area of low pressure, which can cause the trajectory, or path, of the ball to bend or curve. This is known as the Magnus Effect.

Low pressure

Kick is off-center with inside of foot, imparting spin to the ball.

Air flow

Direction of kick

Soccer players also adapt their responses to kicks to accommodate for gravity, the pull of the earth on other objects. All objects have gravity—a force that pulls all matter together. The more mass an object contains, the stronger the pull of gravity. Because the earth contains much more mass than any person or object on it, the planet exerts a force of gravity that pulls smaller things on its surface down toward it.

The force of gravity counteracts an object's tendency to stay in motion in a straight line. When a soccer ball sails into the air, there is a point at which it can rise no farther—the pull of the earth's gravity will overcome the ball's upward motion and start bringing it back down to the ground. Gravity is what makes a ball move in an arc after a hard kick—it rises, and then it begins to come back down to Earth. Experienced soccer players can predict when and where the ball will descend, positioning themselves near the point where it will come back down so they can try to intercept it.

A soccer ball's trajectory, or path of motion, can also be affected by environmental forces, such as wind. If wind and the ball are moving in opposite directions, then the blowing wind will create a force of resistance against the ball—in short, the ball will not go as far unless a player kicks harder to compensate for the force of the wind. Even balls kicked along the ground are subject to resistance in the form of friction, which is a force created whenever two surfaces rub or slide against each other. Soccer balls experience friction when they roll or bounce along the ground, especially from surfaces such as the grass of the playing field. Long grass, which has more surface area, will create more friction, absorb more of the ball's energy, and slow the ball down faster than short grass will.

A soccer player is constantly considering basic facts of physics, such as the laws of motion, gravity's pull on the ball, wind resistance, and friction, throughout a game. "Does the player use physics formulas? Of course not," say engineers Seyed Hamid Hamraz and Seyed Shams Feyzabadi. But, they say, "we can firmly express that the player [does] the job by way of experience."[8] A soccer player's actions are anything but random—they are guided by an innate understanding of physics, mastered through practice.

Keeping the Goal in Sight

Whether a ball will overcome gravity, friction, and the actions of other players to make it into the goal is the big question in soccer. Like the size of the soccer field, the size of the goal boxes is important to the outcome of a soccer match. A standard goal in an adult soccer game is a metal frame 24 feet (7.3m) wide by 8 feet (2.4m) tall. These dimensions give the goalkeeper a fair chance at defending the entire goal and the opposing team a fair chance at getting the ball past the goalkeeper and scoring. "A top-class goalkeeper can cover the whole of the goal given a little more than a second," says Wesson, and a good kicker "can kick the ball at 80 miles per hour [129kmh]."[9] A larger goal box would be too difficult for a goalkeeper to defend, making goals too easy to obtain. A smaller goal box would make it almost impossible for the opposing team to score. Specific dimensions for the goal box help make a soccer game fair for both teams.

A goalkeeper springs to make a save. The standard dimensions of the goal box balance the goalkeeper's ability to effectively cover the area with the opponent's ability to score.

Leveling the Playing Field

There is more to a balanced soccer field than standard measurements and dimensions. To make sure a match is fair, fields must be literally balanced, meaning that they do not slope from one end to the other. They also cannot have hills, dips, or craters. An uneven, unbalanced field can make the game more difficult for one team than the other. It can also lead to added risk of injuries for the players.

Field architects, people who design competitive sports fields, use knowledge of physics to create level playing surfaces that are safe and fair for both teams. First, the area must be mostly flat. A field cannot slope noticeably from side to side, since a slope will affect the movement of the soccer ball. A ball that lands on a flat surface will stay put, but a ball that lands on a slope will begin to roll due to the forces of gravity, and this will affect everything about how the soccer game is played. It may lead to more out-of-bounds kicks, for example, if the ball tends to roll outside the perimeter line of the field. Every time a ball goes out-of-bounds, play must stop while a player throws the ball back in. This interrupts the flow of the game and is frustrating for players and spectators.

Even worse than a field that slopes from side to side is one that slopes from end to end. The team whose goal is on the downhill end of the slope will be at a distinct disadvantage. The players will constantly be fighting the ball's tendency to roll toward their own goal. They will also have to run uphill against the slope as they try to move the ball toward the opposing team's goal. The players on the opposite team, meanwhile, will be working downhill—the ball will naturally roll in their favor, and it will take less physical effort to run toward the opposing team's goal. Even a slight slope, invisible to the naked eye, can make a difference in the efforts of the two teams and in the outcome of a game. Field architects

SOCCER TAKES ALL

207

Number of countries in the world with professional FIFA soccer teams. The United Nations only has 192 member countries.

carefully measure for any slope in the area where they want to build a field. If the field is sloped, dirt must be added or removed to level out the area.

Smoothing the Turf

Just as important as removing a noticeable slope from the field is smoothing out any sudden hills or dips. A soccer player running at full speed and concentrating on other players and the ball may not see an uneven patch of ground and might stumble or trip. Not only will this interrupt the momentum of the game, but a player could also be injured. Therefore, field designers take extra care to make sure that a soccer field is without any uneven areas, such as bumps or craters.

Perfectly flat fields, however, can also pose problems. The physical properties of water and its tendency to puddle can have an effect on the outcome of a soccer game, too. Water that falls on a soccer field during a rainstorm or from sprinklers watering the grass will have nowhere to go. It will form puddles or sheets of water, and these make their own hazards during a soccer game. Water molecules have a tendency to

Young soccer players chase a ball through a puddle. The surface tension created by the puddle and the absorption of water into the ball will slow its movement, thus affecting play.

stick to one another, which is why water molecules form water droplets and why water droplets group together to form puddles. A puddle resists being broken apart, because water molecules naturally cling to each other. Their resistance to being separated creates a force called surface tension, which slows the movement of objects on top of or within a body of water. A soccer ball does not roll well on puddled water because of surface tension, and this makes puddles a hazard in a soccer game. "Wet spots on the turf can literally stop the ball dead," say professional sports field designers Jim Puhalla, Jeff Krans, and Mike Goatley. "Unlike [American] football, in which a team can change strategies when the turf is wet (running the ball more and passing it less, for instance), the game of soccer is more severely restricted when the turf fails to drain effectively."[10]

Whenever a ball rolls through a puddle, water droplets stick to it, and this creates even more problems in a game. The surface of a wet ball that has absorbed a small amount of water is slicker and slightly heavier than a dry ball, and this could affect the players' handling of it. Still another problem with wet fields is that if soccer players step into puddles or soggy areas, they might slip, lose their footing, or miss an important pass or kick. "Each time a soccer player kicks the ball, he or she is by definition standing on one foot in a posture that requires good footing," say Puhalla, Krans, and Goatley. "So evenness of the surface becomes an increasingly important issue for the safety and performance of the athletes."[11]

To prevent water from collecting on soccer fields, field architects design the fields to avoid water buildup. They usually do this by adding an almost unnoticeable hill, or crown, down the center of the field lengthwise. This makes the field slope very slightly at a grade of about 1 to 2 percent from the center toward both sidelines. In other words, for every 12 inches (30cm) of distance across the field from the center crown, the field will slope down about 0.25 inch (0.64cm). With this slight grade, any water that collects on the field will trickle toward the sidelines instead of puddling on the playing surface, but the slope is not enough to affect the rolling of the ball or the running of the players.

Crossing the Line

Referees in a soccer game are responsible for determining when a ball is out-of-bounds. When the ball goes over the sidelines, the team that was not the last to touch the ball throws it back in. Throw-ins usually change which team controls the ball, and they can lead to a goal, so out-of-bounds calls are often hotly contested, especially if it is not obvious that the ball actually crossed the sideline. By official soccer rules, a ball is out-of-bounds if at least half of it rolls over the line. Since soccer is such a fast-moving game, this can be hard to determine. Technology may have found a solution in a ball called the CTRUS, which has a clear covering and is equipped with global positioning system technology and radio-frequency identification so that it lights up when it crosses sidelines. It can also determine when players are off sides (another difficult call for referees), and it even records velocity and force of kicks. The CTRUS is not yet used in official games, but in the future, this invention might eliminate the problem of incorrect referee calls in soccer.

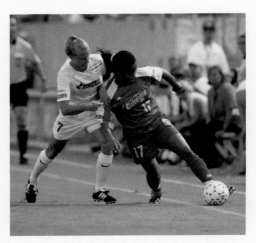

A player dribbles the soccer ball out of bounds while a referee looks on to make the call. The sport is experimenting with technology that equips the ball to light up when it crosses the sideline, thus eliminating the chance of referee error.

Eye on the Ball

The laws of physics do not just affect the way architects design playing fields. Physics properties are also critical to the key component of the game—the ball. A soccer ball is in nearly constant motion during a match as it is kicked, nudged, bumped off of heads, and caught by the goalkeeper. The ball's physical properties are designed specifically for the types of activities soccer players undertake during a game.

The dimensions of soccer balls have changed little since the first official soccer rules were written in the 1860s. Players realized that there is an optimal size and weight for a ball. Balls that are too heavy are cumbersome to kick, and a heavy ball may cause head or neck injuries if players use their heads to stop and redirect it. A ball that is too light, on the other hand, may not travel as players expect. It is much more vulnerable to wind resistance on a blustery day, for example. Bowling balls would be too heavy for use in a soccer game, and beach balls would not be heavy enough. These examples demonstrate why mass (the amount of matter within an object of a certain size) and weight (the amount of gravitational pull the earth has on an object due to its mass) are important characteristics for a soccer ball.

Even slight differences in size or weight can change the way a ball travels across the ground or through the air and could make a pass fall short of its target or a goal shot fly wide of its mark. Therefore, standard weight and circumference measurements for soccer balls were established in the 1860s and have remained unchanged to this day. A standard soccer ball for adult use must weigh between 14 and 16 ounces (397g and 454g), and its circumference, the distance across the widest portion of the sphere, must be between 27 and 28 inches (68.6cm and 71.1cm). These specifications are important because players expect a standard soccer ball to behave a certain way when kicked, dribbled, or bounced off the head. Similar to a field that has not been designed according to official regulations, a ball that has not been made according to official dimensions may change the flow or even the entire outcome of a game. "In football, it is not just the eleven players on the pitch who make the difference between victory and defeat," says Ottmar Hitzfeld, coach of the Swiss national soccer team. "There are other pieces of the puzzle that have to slot together."[12] The ball is one of those pieces.

Building a Ball

Soccer balls have had the same measurements since the 1860s, but they have not always been constructed the same way. In the early 1900s, balls were made from strips of leather stitched together in six panels of three strips each. The panels were sewn inside out, leaving one small opening for the cover to be inverted so that the rough edges of the seams were on the inside of the ball and the outer surface was smooth. After being turned inside out, the finished cover was stuffed with a rubber bladder that could be inflated with air through a rubber stem, and the final opening was laced or stitched together. These balls lost air quickly because they were not sealed tightly at the seams, especially not where the opening at the stem had to be laced or stitched together by hand. The balls usually had to be reinflated at least once during a soccer match. The leather also had a tendency to absorb water on wet fields, so by the end of a game the ball was often very heavy. Many players sustained head and neck injuries from trying to bounce a waterlogged leather ball off their heads.

Not only were the six-paneled leather balls unforgiving in wet weather and quick to deflate, but they were also not precisely round. The leather strips, when stitched together into panels, formed a roughly spherical shape, but the panels themselves created a series of flat segments all over the surface of the ball. These made the ball wobble rather than roll smoothly across a flat surface. Passing and dribbling were challenging when an uneven ball rolled off in a surprising direction because of its uneven shape, as often happened in early games. By the mid–twentieth century, both problems—the ball's unwieldy leather surface and the nonuniform shape—were resolved by new scientific discoveries. One of the most significant was a ball design adopted from the work of an architect named Richard Buckminster Fuller who built geometric dome structures to save on building materials. His idea of using a combination of pentagons (five-sided figures) and hexagons (six-sided figures) to make a domed building was also the answer to soccer-ball manufacturers' troubles.

By stitching together thirty-two small panels, twenty hexagons and twelve

Early soccer balls were made of strips of leather stitched together and sealed with laces after being inflated.

pentagons, and then filling the shape with air to "bulge out" the pentagons and hexagons, designers arrived at a nearly perfect sphere that resisted air leaks. Compared to eighteen flat strips of leather that could not be sewn together into a perfectly round shape with no flat sides, the dome pattern of thirty-two panels of hexagons and pentagons curved smoothly and created no awkward flat areas on the surface of the ball. Having more panels required smaller, tighter seams, as well, which reduced the amount of air that leaked out of the ball. With the pentagons in black and the hexagons in white, the new soccer ball design also took on its traditional coloring, a checkerboard pattern that allowed players to better see the speed and direction of a ball's spin while

THE JABULANI

The official 2010 World Cup soccer ball is called the Jabulani which means "to celebrate" in Zulu – one of the main languages spoken in South Africa, where the tournament was held. The eleven colors of the ball represent the eleven official South African languages.

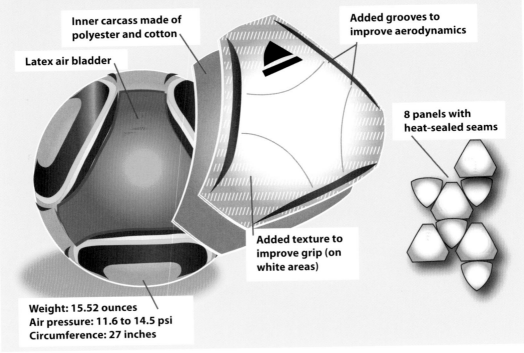

Inner carcass made of polyester and cotton

Added grooves to improve aerodynamics

Latex air bladder

8 panels with heat-sealed seams

Added texture to improve grip (on white areas)

Weight: 15.52 ounces
Air pressure: 11.6 to 14.5 psi
Circumference: 27 inches

it was airborne. The design, called the Buckyball, was officially accepted by the professional soccer world during the 1970 World Cup and long stood as the standard soccer ball design around the world. It was replaced in the 2006 and 2010 World Cups by new balls with heat-sealed seams and better aerodynamic properties.

Improved ball designs did nothing to fix waterlogged balls on the playing field, however. The solution for that problem came about in the 1960s, with the discovery of synthetic materials. By the 1980s, synthetic balls, usually made of a mix of polyurethane and polyvinyl chloride (PVC), had replaced the leather kind. They were smooth, sturdy, and unlike leather, almost completely waterproof. Today's soccer balls are made of a synthetic surface, or casing, filled with a latex air bladder. Balls used in professional leagues must meet very harsh standards, including weight, circumference, bounce, pressure loss, and balance. To be a candidate for a World Cup match, a brand of ball must undergo strict laboratory tests that include being flung two thousand times against a steel plate at 31 miles per hour (50kmh). Only ball designs that retain their shape, balance, and air pressure after these tests are recommended for professional games. "The quality of the ball, as the heart of the game, is decisive,"[13] says retired professional and World Cup soccer referee Urs Meier.

The Stage Is Set

The dimensions of the field, the size of the goal boxes, and the design of the ball are all critical to the outcome of a soccer match. All of these elements and the scientific properties that contribute to them, such as the physics of objects in motion and how air and water resistance affect them, have helped shape the game of soccer as we know it today. The truly essential components of a soccer game, however, are the people playing it. The field is merely the stage for the performance, the ball a prop. The real show does not happen until the players step onto the field, using their bodies as biomechanical tools carrying out one of the most complex physical achievements of the human body—participation in a game where the use of hands is almost entirely forbidden.

CHAPTER 3

Look! No Hands!
The Biomechanics
of Playing Soccer

It was 1986, and the World Cup was in full swing. In the quarterfinals, Argentina faced off in a game against England. Argentina's Diego Maradona received a pass about 66 yards (60m) from England's goal, and he was off like a rocket. He dribbled, sprinted, and evaded one England defender after another, rapidly closing in on the goal. The goalkeeper surged toward Maradona but stumbled. Maradona never lost an instant of momentum as he dodged the final line of defense and kicked the ball into the net, scoring a game-winning goal. Argentina went on to win the 1986 World Cup. Maradona's nearly half-field dash was dubbed the goal of the century, helping to cement his reputation as one of the best soccer players of all time.

Maradona did more than just score a goal that day. What made his solitary charge up the field so amazing was the way he pulled together so many different skills and movements into one dramatic play. He combined sprinting, dodging, balance, and kicking with a simultaneous observation of everyone and everything around him on the field. He linked multiple physical abilities of the human body into one fluid shot at the goal. Like so many of the most famous moments

Argentina's Diego Maradona makes an impressive drive to the goal on his way to scoring the game-winning goal in the World Cup quarterfinal match against England in 1986.

in soccer history, Maradona's goal of the century was a case study in biomechanics—the field of science that examines how laws of physics and mechanics are put to work in biological human performance, especially in sports. Soccer, unlike most sports, limits the use of the arms and hands, so the mechanics of human movement—things like leverage, center of gravity, and balance—must be developed without the use of hands, to the best of a player's ability. The greatest moments in soccer happen when players have mastered biomechanics and, like Maradona, transform their bodies into well-tuned machines that never miss a step.

Anatomy of a Kick: The Legs as Levers

Soccer is mostly a kicking game, a sport dominated by the work of the legs and feet. It is called football in most countries of the world for a good reason—the foot is what comes in contact most often with the ball. However, in terms of mechanics, the foot is merely the end of the leg. With every kick of the ball, the foot functions like the snapping tip of a whip, but the whip itself—the entire leg—drives every kick, whether large or small.

A Game for the Ages

In the South African village of Nkowankowa soccer is the favorite pastime of an unlikely group of citizens, who call their team Vakhegula Vakhegula, which means "Grandmother Grandmother" in Tsonga, the local language. Elderly women, some in their eighties, cast off their traditional skirts for soccer uniforms and shoes, and they play the game in spite of cultural beliefs that they should not because of their age, their gender, their health, and their community's traditions. All around the world, people of retirement age are finding a similar attraction to soccer and making headlines. In 2001 in Germany, Kurt Meyer won that country's Goal of the Year contest by vote of television viewers who had watched him sink a ball into the net from an almost impossible angle. Meyer was in his eighties, but his goal beat out amazing plays that year by many of the country's younger, faster, professional soccer players. Athletes like Meyer and the South African team of grandmothers show that soccer is truly a game for the people, no matter their age, gender, or status in life.

A group of elderly South African women make up a soccer team called Vakhegula Vakhegula ("Grandmother Grandmother"), an example of how the sport is enjoyed by players of all ages.

REVERSE TREND

0.6 miles (1 km)

Average distance a professional soccer goalkeeper walks backward during a game.

In soccer, the human leg works as a system of levers—straight bars that rotate around a fixed point, or fulcrum, to apply force to another point (in this case, the ball). The straight bones of the leg—the femur in the thigh and the tibia and fibula that make up the shin—act as the bars of the lever. The points around which they rotate are the joints—the hip, knee, and ankle. Both portions of the leg, upper and lower, act as separate but related levers during a kick, combining their force and direction to make the foot connect with the ball with particular power or precision. Because the hip joint can rotate, it can move the upper leg not just backward and forward but diagonally and from side to side. The knee joint moves only forward and backward, but combined with the variety of angles possible at the hip, both joints work together to create a lever that can contact the ball from limitless directions and with various amounts of force.

Controlling the direction and force of the leg and foot at the moment of a kick is the central skill of soccer. The velocity, or speed, of the ball is related to the force used to move it—the strength of the kick. A good soccer player at the professional level has the ability to kick the ball an average of 35 to 38 yards (32m to 35m) per second, but kicking that hard is not always an advantage. A ball that sails past its intended target—a teammate or the goal—does no good to anyone in a soccer game. Most soccer kicks, in fact, are designed to achieve a velocity that is well below what powerful kickers could achieve if they gave it their all. "Most of the actions and maneuvers in soccer situations are executed with submaximal force and velocity, but with greater accuracy and purposefulness," says Pekka Luhtanen of the Research Institute for Olympic Sports. "Accuracy in kicking [is] the highest when the velocity of the ball [is] 80% of the maximal velocity."[14] Often just a mere tap of the ball is needed, such as when players dribble, making short kicks to keep the ball in front of them as they run up the field.

THE MECHANICS OF A KICK

Hamstring flexed

1 As the player approaches for a kick with the right leg, the left foot is planted next to the ball for support while the right hamstring is flexed to bring the leg back and upwards.

2 Once the leg is raised, the right hip flexor and quadriceps are engaged to powerfully bring the leg downwards, where the foot makes contact with the soccer ball.

Right hip flexor

Quadriceps

Quadriceps

Right hip flexor

3 In the phase known as the follow-through, the player's right hip flexor and quadriceps flex to bring the leg forward and upwards, transferring energy into the ball and completing the kick.

Flexing Power

A soccer player's ability to apply just the right amount of force to the ball is controlled by muscles. Muscles are attached to and control the movement of bones, or in the case of kicking, the direction and force of the lever system created by the legs. The quadriceps is the large muscle running down the front of the thigh. Along the back of the thigh is the hamstring, and where the femur bone of the thigh connects to the hip is the hip flexor muscle. These are the three major muscles responsible for moving the leg in a soccer kick.

The biomechanical action of a full-force kick happens like this: First, the soccer player plants one foot on the ground as support. This frees up the opposite leg to work as the kicking lever. The player then extends the kicking leg as far back as possible, because the larger the swing of the lever, the more speed and energy the foot can gain and the more forceful the kick will be. Once the leg is extended backward, the hip flexor muscle at the front of the hip tenses to pull the thigh forward. The knee is bent at first, lessening the amount of friction placed on the leg due to air resistance. This allows the thigh to reach the highest possible speed during the downswing. When the knee is positioned over the ball, the hamstring muscle along the back of the thigh, which has been tensed to pull the lower leg backward, releases its tension. The powerful quadriceps, meanwhile, tenses to pull the lower leg and the foot forward. The shin swings down like a whip, and the foot, anchored by a stiff ankle so it works like the heavy end of a club, transfers the combined energy of the entire leg to its target, the ball.

The kick works like a chain reaction, gathering strength and momentum from the start of the backswing to the instant of impact, when the kinetic energy of the leg is transferred to the ball to power it into motion. The kick is the most familiar biomechanical application in the game of soccer.

Trapping: Newton's Third Law in Action

Kicking is the main action most people associate with soccer, but stopping the movement of a ball that has been kicked is just as important, because it allows players to intercept passes or keep the ball out of the goal. Stopping a moving soccer ball is known as trapping, and it involves different biomechanics than kicking it. The kick involves transferring

A Zambian player leaps to trap a ball with his chest in order to stop its trajectory and gain control over where it goes next.

energy to the ball to make it move, but the trap involves absorbing a moving ball's energy to slow it down.

Newton's first and second laws of motion state that a resting object stays still unless a force moves it, and whenever a certain amount of force is applied to an object, it will move predictably. Both are important concepts for soccer players, since they are the reason a soccer ball must be kicked with a certain amount of force in order for it to move the way players want it to. Newton's third law of motion is also very important in soccer, however. This law states that for every action, there is an equal and opposition reaction. Actions and reactions always occur in equal pairs. Whenever a moving soccer ball hits a solid surface, for example, the ball exerts a force on the surface at the moment of impact. The surface also exerts its own equal force back against the ball. If the solid surface has a greater mass than the ball, the opposite force it exerts will cause the ball to bounce away in the opposite direction.

This concept of opposite reactions is critical in soccer, because when players are not dribbling or passing the ball, they are usually trying to trap it, placing themselves in front of it to stop its progress and make it fall to their feet so they can control it. "Usually a player moves around a soccer field without the ball," says soccer coach and physical education professor Danny Mielke. "When a ball arrives, that player wants to make the most of the situation by controlling the ball with a superb trap, then choose to either continue play through a dribble or pass or shoot the ball."[15] Since no soccer player other than the goalie can use hands to catch the ball, stopping the ball's progress means placing some part of the body—the chest, the knee, the foot, the thigh, or even the head—directly in the path of the moving ball. But Newton's third law of motion predicts that when a moving ball strikes another object that has greater mass, such as a human leg or torso, the ball will tend to bounce off and move the other way. To effectively trap a soccer ball and keep control of it, soccer players use special techniques to counteract Newton's third law of motion.

The trick to successfully trapping a moving ball is to absorb its energy. A soccer ball will not bounce off a flexible surface, such as a pillow, the same way it will bounce off a hard surface, such as a brick wall. At the moment of impact, the flexible surface will move a little in the direction the ball is already going. The surface acts as a cushion, sinking in slightly to absorb some of the ball's force when the two objects collide. This will reduce the ball's tendency to bounce the opposite way. The wall, on the other hand, will not flex at the moment of collision. It will not cushion the impact or absorb the ball's energy, so the ball's movement in the opposite direction after the impact will be greater. To trap a ball, then, soccer players must try to cushion it—to absorb some of the moving ball's energy at the moment of impact. They do this by allowing their chest, thigh, knee, foot, or other body

Mama Mia

Known all over the world as one of the best female soccer players in history, Mia Hamm holds numerous records and has one of the largest fan bases of any American athlete. Standing only 5 feet, 5 inches tall, the slender scorer was formidable on the soccer field during her seventeen-year career. At age fifteen, she became the youngest player ever chosen for the U.S. national team and was a much-feared striking phenomenon for more than a decade, leading the U.S. women's soccer team to a World Cup victory in 1999 and to gold medals at the 1996 and 2004 Olympics. Hamm was twice named FIFA World Player of the Year (2001 and 2002), and she and her teammate Michelle Akers are the only two women (and the only Americans) named on the FIFA's list of the 125 greatest living soccer players. When Hamm retired from soccer in 2004, she started the Mia Hamm Foundation to raise money for bone marrow transplant patients. Her interest in helping bone marrow patients is due to her brother: He died of a bone marrow disease in 1997. Hamm is also an outspoken advocate of girls' involvement in sports.

American soccer player Mia Hamm celebrates a goal during the 2000 Olympics. She is considered one of the top female players in the history of the game.

part to move a little in the same direction the ball is already going. This way, when the ball connects with a player's body, most of its energy is absorbed, not deflected. The ball will drop to the ground near the player's feet instead of bouncing away toward opponents who could steal it. This makes the trap an essential technique for soccer players to master.

Staying Centered

To effectively trap a soccer ball by moving in the direction it is already going, the body's center of gravity becomes important. Every object has a center of gravity, or single point at which the bulk of its weight and mass are located. The motion of any object can be described as the motion of its center of gravity from one place to another. Objects also turn or rotate around their center of gravity. So when soccer players attempt to receive a ball, they not only gauge the *ball's* center of gravity and where it will land with the greatest force, they must also understand their *own* center of gravity—how and where they need to position themselves so they can absorb the force of the ball.

Center of gravity is closely tied to balance. Objects with a low center of gravity have their center point of weight and mass positioned close to the ground—in general, these are broader, flatter objects that would be difficult to knock over. The higher the center of gravity, the easier it is for an object to topple. Young trees are a good example of how the center of gravity works. If a tree is tall and wispy, its center of gravity is higher off the ground. A strong wind will cause it to bend or even break. But if the tree is short and solid, its center of gravity is low to the ground, and it is less likely to bend in the wind. Even if the two trees have the exact same weight and mass, the one with the lower center of gravity will be more difficult to knock over.

Soccer players use the same type of concept during a game, especially when they trap a ball. They may bend their knees slightly to lower their center of gravity so that they can absorb the ball's impact with their body. If their center of gravity is too high, a forcefully kicked ball might knock them off balance when they try to trap it. Good soccer players have an innate understanding of center of gravity and use it to their advantage on the field, helping them to move side to side to trap a ball or to change direction in an instant. "Athletes that need to be able to turn quickly know to keep their center of gravity low," says civil engineer Cameron Bauer. "When their legs and feet move their bodies, moments [of opportunity] are created about their center of gravity."[16] By keeping their center of gravity low, players are better able to change direction while maintaining their balance. Center of gravity is one of the most important elements of biomechanics in soccer.

Heading the Ball

Soccer players also use their center of gravity to help make up for the fact that they cannot use their hands. They instead fine-tune their ability to move their entire body toward a ball to stop or redirect its progress. One of the most unique skills in soccer is the use of the head to stop or move the ball. Like

A Jordanian player uses her head to redirect the ball, rising to her toes to use the full force of her body.

the act of kicking, where the weakest part of the leg—the foot—is what contacts the ball, the act of heading transfers force from a stronger part of the body—the trunk, made up of the back and chest—up through the neck to the striking point, the forehead. Often, the player jumps into the air to make contact with the ball in order to increase the movement, or swing, of the lever mechanism created by the torso, neck, and head. Most headers actually involve most of the body. "The action of the body in heading has been compared to that of a catapult," says Luhtanen. "Force is produced by strong contraction of the trunk flexors, hip flexors, and knee extensors prior to impact."[17]

Using the head as a primary striking force seems as if it would cause serious injury, but heading is relatively safe because players train themselves to contract their neck muscles so that the neck and head themselves are not whipped forward but act as a stiff, clubbing surface. Experienced

A New Field in Soccer

Soccer is called the people's game, but that does not stop some nonhuman players from trying out their skills on the pitch. Every year since 1997, teams from around the world have faced off during the RoboCup, a soccer tournament for robots. Divided into different leagues, such as small size, middle size, four legged, and humanoid, the players rely on artificial intelligence, camera vision, and the quality of their mechanical construction to pass and intercept a soccer ball, defend their own goal, and try to score against the other team. RoboCup is not nearly as popular as the World Cup among the general population, but in the field of robotics, designing and building a soccer team that wins a RoboCup title is the ultimate honor. RoboCup players still lag far behind humans in speed, reflexes, and mental processing, but that could change in the future. Robot scientists predict that by the year 2050, RoboCup-level players will be so advanced that they will be able to compete against human soccer teams—and they might even win.

soccer players suffer few head and neck injuries from heading the ball, despite the fact that headers are frequent in soccer matches. "Heading is an important skill . . . for advancing the ball downfield, intercepting a pass, or as a shot on goal," says Luhtanen, and in elite soccer matches, "a large percentage of the goals are scored from headers."[18] Headers are an important way for soccer players to move the ball without using their hands.

All Hands on Deck

Soccer is not a game played without *any* use of hands whatsoever. The rules state that hands and arms cannot be used by players other than the goalkeeper to catch the ball, change its direction, or push or grab other players. Yet, when soccer players are in action on the field, their hands and arms do not remain stiffly at their sides. Even though the arms do not actually contact the ball, they are used in almost every kick, header, and jump in the game. For one thing, arms held out to the sides help balance the body around its center of gravity, because having an equal amount of weight on both sides of the torso adds breadth to the body overall and makes it more difficult for gravity to topple it over. This is why it is easier to walk along a balance beam with the arms lifted away from the body and why arms held out to the sides act as a balancing mechanism when a soccer player is preparing to kick the ball. When the arms are swung from side to side, they also give energy to a twisting motion of the upper body to add power to a spinning jump or kick. The arms are used in soccer during headers, too. They help the player keep her balance, and when swung in a front-to-back motion, the arms add momentum and force to the forward motion of the torso during a header.

Whenever the ball rolls out-of-bounds in a soccer game, hands are important, too. A game stops momentarily while a player throws the ball back into play, usually by gripping the ball with both hands, bringing the arms back over the head, and flinging the ball back onto the field. A properly executed throw-in is often critical to a successful soccer game. "Restarts, or dead-ball situations, provide some of the best

A player prepares for a throw-in after a ball has rolled out of bounds, bringing his arms over his head to fling the ball forcefully onto the field.

opportunities in soccer to create goal-scoring chances," says Gene Klein, a coach with the United States Soccer Federation. At the same time, a botched toss from the sidelines can be intercepted by the opposing team, leading to a score. "Games can be won or lost in these situations,"[19] says Klein.

Nowhere on the soccer field are hands as important, however, as in the goal box. The goalkeeper is the one player on a soccer team allowed to use any part of the body that will help keep the ball out of the goal. The goalkeeper may kick, trap, and even head a ball if that is the best way to stop the other team from scoring. Goalkeepers are notorious for their ability to leap, dive, and tumble in order to catch a high, low, or fast-moving ball and stop the threat of a score. They do this by instantaneously understanding and using principles of biomechanics and laws of motion. "Top goalkeepers have what we call soft hands," say Peter Mellor, goalkeeper coach of the 2003 U.S. national soccer team, and Tony Waiters, a former soccer player and coach. "They seem to be able to absorb the ball, holding most shots and catching most crosses [shots that come into the goal at an angle]." Goalkeepers, they say, "always know where they are in the game, tactically."[20] Within the goal box of a soccer match, elegant and impressive athletic uses of the hands occur.

Mastering the Mechanics

Good soccer players use biomechanics effortlessly, but their mastery of these skills does not occur overnight. Years of learning and practice are behind every amazing soccer move spectators watch on the field or on TV. Soccer players seem to respond to the needs of the game mechanically, without even needing to think about what they are doing. In the best players, part of this skill may come naturally. Yet, any player can improve at the game of soccer by exercising the body in certain ways, training it to respond more quickly and naturally to the specific kinds of tasks often required in soccer.

CHAPTER 4

The Right Condition: Physical Training for Soccer Players

In many sports, there is an ideal body shape or size among professional athletes. Players in the National Basketball Association, for example, have an average height of about 6 feet, 7 inches, and one of the tallest players in the league, Yao Ming of the Houston Rockets, is 7 feet, 6 inches tall. In the Women's National Basketball Association, the average height of players is about 6 feet, but the tallest players are well over that—Margo Dydek, now retired, holds the record as the tallest player in women's professional basketball history at 7 feet, 2 inches tall. The average height for a man in the United States is 5 feet, 9 inches, and the average U.S. woman is 5 feet, 4 inches tall. Basketball is one sport in which tall players are typical.

Most men who play American football are bigger than average, as well. In the National Football League, the average player weighs about 250 pounds (113kg). Offensive tackles, who try to hold back the opposing team's defense, are usually the heaviest players on a team, and most at the professional level weigh more than 300 pounds (136kg). Professional football players are bulkier than the average American man, who weighs about 190 pounds (86kg). Bulky, muscular bodies have become so standard in American football that slender players are at a physical disadvantage in the game. The sport is dominated by men, who tend to be larger and stronger than women and can typically overpower them in a sport that requires full body contact. Although women do play tackle football professionally in the Independent Women's Football League, no woman has ever been drafted to play with men in the National Football League.

There is nothing a short person can do to grow taller, and although bodybuilding exercises can help a person gain muscle mass and bulk, there may be limits to how much mass an average person can gain. Certain sports are better suited to players with certain body types. This is not true in soccer, however. One reason soccer is often called the people's game is that it can be played by almost anyone, regardless of their size. "Soccer is the Everyman Sport," says physician Richard Witzig. "There is no perfect soccer body . . . one of the equities of soccer is that unique individuals, short or tall, stout or slim, have excelled at the highest level. Players need only have well-developed lower extremities (from hip to foot), coordination and endurance."[21] World Cup–level soccer players can be slim like U.S. midfielder José Torres at 5 feet, 7 inches and 135 pounds (61kg) or large like U.S. goalkeeper Marcus Hahnemann at 6 feet, 3 inches and 220 pounds (100kg). Women players range from slender, like the United States' famous soccer forward Mia Hamm at 5 feet, 5 inches and 125 pounds (57kg), to larger than average, like Germany's Birgit Prinz, who stands 5 feet, 10 inches tall and weighs 163 pounds (74kg). Great soccer players come in all sizes.

People of any stature can learn to play soccer, but this does not mean the sport is easy. During a typical soccer game, says college soccer coach Ron McEachen, "players run up to nine miles, do upwards of 200 sprints of varying distances, kick the ball 75 to 100 times, and jump to head the ball as many as 100 times. It's a physical game in which players make full-speed contact with each other as often as

Soccer Warrior

Few soccer players show the physical toll the sport can have on the body like former soccer phenomenon Michelle Akers. Her fifteen-year professional career began in 1985 with the U.S. women's first-ever international match and ended in 2000 after punishing her with a long list of physical ailments and trauma. Akers nonetheless played the game more fiercely than any woman in soccer history, scoring 105 goals in international matches and helping her team to two World Cup championship titles and an Olympic gold medal. On top of being battered with serious physical injuries that ranged from joint damage to broken facial bones, Akers also had chronic fatigue syndrome, a long-term condition that results in extreme physical weakness. The illness sapped her body of the strength to sit up some days and caused severe migraine headaches. Yet Akers continued playing soccer for several years after her diagnosis, despite eventually requiring intravenous medication after games. When she retired from soccer at age thirty-four, she told reporters, "I have huge peace in knowing I fought to the very end and have nothing else to give." Akers left a legacy as one of the most dedicated players, male or female, in the history of the sport.

Quoted in Sylvia R. J. Scott. "Michelle Akers: A Conquering Spirit—Living with Chronic Fatigue Syndrome." *Healthy & Natural Journal*, February 2001, http://www.highbeam.com/doc/1G1-76445410.html.

50 times a game."[22] Soccer requires both excellent physical fitness and a great deal of technical skill. Whether tall or short, heavily muscled or slim, players train hard to develop the coordination, muscle strength, endurance, and flexibility that will propel them through a physically difficult match.

Do Not Look Down

One of the essential skills in most sports is hand-eye coordination. The eyes constantly receive visual stimuli and send information about what they see to the brain. The brain in turn sends signals to the body through the central nervous system, the body's information gathering, processing, and control system, to respond to visual stimuli. How accurately and quickly the hands reach for, grab, or manipulate an object once the eyes have seen it is a measure of hand-eye coordination. The ability to catch and throw a ball, for example, is second nature for most athletes, and the best can do it without ever looking at their hands—their brain intuitively measures the speed and the direction of an approaching ball and positions their hands perfectly for a catch. This is something soccer goalkeepers, for example, can do with amazing accuracy.

A slightly different skill is also needed in soccer: foot-eye coordination. It works much the same way as hand-eye coordination in that the feet have to respond quickly to what the eyes see. Foot-eye coordination is essential for basic tasks, like running or climbing stairs, neither of which is easy to do with the eyes closed—the brain needs information from the eyes in order to direct the movement of the legs and feet. In soccer, foot-eye coordination is fundamental for kicking, dribbling, or trapping a ball. The best soccer players are even said to develop eyes on their feet. The Brazilian soccer star known as Pelé, widely considered the best soccer player of all time, recalls advice he was given very early in his soccer-playing years: "If you ever want to be a decent player, you have to learn to use each foot equally. Without stopping to think about it. It has to be automatic."[23] Soccer training includes drills like dribbling with the soles of the feet or kicking a ball repeatedly against a wall and intercepting it on the rebound to develop the foot-eye coordination that the world's best soccer players have mastered.

Balance and Reflexes

The brain's coordination of body movement in response to visual stimuli allows soccer players to control the ball. It also guides their balance and reflexes. Balance is an essential soccer skill closely tied to foot-eye coordination. A soccer ball can move more than 100 miles per hour (161kmh) at the professional level and changes direction constantly as it gets passed from player to player. Running at full speed, soccer players keep their eyes on the ball and often must change direction in an instant without losing their balance. Balancing is a complicated process involving fluid levels in the inner ear that shift as the body moves. The ears send information about fluid levels back to the brain, which combines this information with what the eyes are seeing and signals the muscles to move in a way that restores balance and prevents falling down. By practicing the same movements over and over, athletes can train their bodies to respond more quickly to what their eyes see and to changing fluid levels in their ears during movements that are common to their sport. Over time and with a lot of practice, soccer players' bodies get used to making abrupt turns in response to the movement of the ball without toppling over at a critical moment in the game.

Coordination between the hands, feet, and eyes also relates to reflexes. A reflex is an involuntary, instantaneous response to a stimulus—something heard, seen, or felt. Blinking when an object flies toward one's face is an example of a reflex. A person with slow reflexes may not even flinch or duck if an object were to fly at his face. A person with faster reflexes might have time to duck or put her hands up to deflect the object. An athlete with well-trained reflexes will catch it. It is possible to develop reflexes to respond more quickly to stimuli, especially visual ones. Improving coordination between the eyes, hands, and feet, for example, also improves reflexes. Practicing any activity that requires coordination between the hands, feet, and eyes helps athletes to develop better reflexes. Soccer drills to improve players' reflexes include having two players face off on the field. One prepares to kick the ball, and the other cannot move until the ball is in motion. The second player then must react quickly to intercept the moving ball. The closer the players stand to one another, the harder this drill will be and the better reflexes it will require. Common soccer drills also include tasks like dribbling a ball between plastic cones to improve foot-eye coordination. The more time spent practicing such activities, as well as playing actual soccer games, the better a player's reflexes will become. Most professional soccer players have practiced drills like these regularly since childhood, so their reflexes are well honed.

A young soccer player practices dribbling a ball around a cone in order to develop his foot-eye coordination, balance, and reflexes.

Staying Strong

Developing good coordination and reflexes helps soccer players fine-tune their skills and lends grace and finesse to their style of play, but even before they start to master these important aspects of the game, soccer players must get their bodies in the right physical shape to handle the rigors of a soccer match. They need to be able to kick a soccer ball powerfully, for example. They also must be able to do things like jog, turn, leap to head the soccer ball, and break into a sprint throughout the full ninety minutes of a match without becoming exhausted or losing focus. To carry out these

Members of the Japan national team practice before World Cup play in 2010. Their strong, developed leg muscles provide them with balance and kicking power.

tasks, soccer players focus on two important aspects of fitness—strength and endurance.

Muscles give the body its strength and are the driving force behind any athletic performance. There are three types of muscle tissue: cardiac, smooth, and skeletal. Cardiac muscle tissue is found in the heart, and smooth muscle tissue lines some of the internal organs. These types of muscle tissue are not controlled voluntarily (the heart, for example, beats whether a person thinks about it or not). Skeletal muscle tissue, on the other hand, *is* controlled voluntarily. Skeletal muscles are connected to bones to power the body's movement. They consist of muscle fibers that stretch and relax, something like a cluster of rubber bands. Skeletal muscles can be strengthened and made bigger through exercise.

Developing large, strong skeletal muscles is an ongoing process that happens by gently overworking a specific muscle or muscle group until the fibers of muscle tissue become slightly damaged. The body quickly repairs the muscle tissue, making it a little hardier in the process to withstand further use. Within a couple of days after being overused, the muscle tissue will not only be healed, but it will also be slightly larger and stronger than before. Over time, as an athlete repeatedly breaks down skeletal muscle tissue and allows it to heal, muscles grow in mass and strength.

For soccer players, developing strong leg muscles is important for everything from kicking to maintaining balance during a game. "Players who get knocked off the ball or land on the ground need to improve their footwork and the strength of their hamstrings and quadriceps to enhance their balance," says McEachen. "The true test is if a player can maintain a good base of support in all situations while competing."[24] Muscular legs not only bring better balance but also more powerful kicks. Large muscles are heavier than small muscles. Since the leg acts like a club during a kick, a heavier leg will swing harder and contact the ball with more force. Strong, bulky legs are often an advantage for soccer players. During training, a soccer player may concentrate on adding bulk to the lower body using weightlifting techniques to develop the quadriceps on the front of the thigh and the hamstrings along the back of the thigh.

Being *exceptionally* bulky, however, can be a disadvantage in soccer. Precisely because muscle tissue is so heavy, soccer players should not have too much of it weighing down their legs. A soccer game requires a great deal of running. Toting muscular legs that are twice as heavy as every other players' could affect another crucial aspect of a soccer player's physical fitness—endurance, or the ability to remain physically active for long periods without tiring out.

DON'T SWEAT IT

2 to 3 pints (0.95L to 1.42L)

Amount of sweat that the average adult body produces per hour during vigorous exercise, which is equivalent to 2 to 3 pounds (0.9kg to 1.4kg) of body weight.

The Long Run

Superior endurance, probably more than any other physical ability, is the hallmark of soccer. Teams whose players can tolerate intense physical activity from the beginning of a soccer match to the end improve their chances of winning. Teams whose players are exhausted and gasping for air by the end of a match may not fare as well. Just as athletes train their muscles to become bigger and stronger, they also train to improve endurance. They may begin training by jogging long distances, for example, to prepare their bodies to run the equivalent of several miles in every game. However, soccer is not played in a continuous jog but in repeated bursts of sprinting, broken up by periods of walking, trotting, jumping, and even running backward. Soccer players must develop stamina for these demanding activities.

The ability of the muscles to produce bursts of speed even when the body becomes tired is important in soccer. Repeated sprints are a form of *anaerobic* exercise—exercise that uses up the oxygen normally needed by a working muscle, forcing the muscle to break down carbohydrates

Members of the United States women's national soccer team run laps as part of their practice routine in order to develop stamina to sustain them through a full game.

for energy. This process is called glycolysis, and it creates a byproduct called lactic acid, which builds up in the muscles and makes them feel sore and tired. Every time a muscle is used anaerobically, however, it becomes stronger and better adapted to the activity. Endurance training that demands many short sprints helps a soccer player build muscles that can handle the repeated anaerobic demands of a soccer game. "The endurance of a soccer athlete is

Jabulani

During the 2010 World Cup Tournament, goalkeepers on the world's best teams faced the most fearsome adversary in soccer history, faster and trickier than any they had met before. Their foe was named Jabulani—the official soccer ball of the 2010 World Cup. Designed by the Adidas company, Jabulani (roughly meaning "to celebrate" in Zulu, an African language) was streamlined with thermally bonded seams to be perfectly round and faster than any ball before it. The surface was circled with "grip 'n groove" texturing intended to give players a more stable kicking experience and to ensure a smooth, powerful path through the air. Jabulani also had a superior ability to curve in flight, something goalkeepers dislike because they cannot predict what the ball will do. Many other players also disliked the ball's unpredictability. Jabulani veered away from its intended target during passes and goal shots and sailed over players jumping up to try to head it. The ball may have contributed to the low number of goals scored during the tournament's opening matches, the lowest

accuracy rate of goal shots in World Cup history. As of early 2011 soccer officials have not decided if the ball will be used in future World Cup tournaments, but Adidas still makes and sells the Jabulani, which costs about $150.

The official soccer ball of the 2010 World Cup was called the Jabulani. Some players thought that design features meant to improve play actually made it more difficult to use.

more than just being able to run forever," say major league U.S. soccer coaches Sigi Schmid and Bob Alejo. "A high level of endurance will allow the soccer athlete to maintain nearly perfect execution of skills at close to 100 percent effort throughout a match."[25] Consistently using muscles in the right way and pushing slightly past one's comfort level at every practice are how soccer players improve endurance for peak performance during a game.

Feeding the Muscles

Soccer players who can endure difficult physical demands depend on more than strong muscles. Even the fittest of players will be limited in their abilities if they do not eat properly and drink enough liquid, because the body depends on having the right types and amounts of nutrients and fluids in order to work efficiently. An athlete's body requires a constant store of carbohydrates, for example, because living cells convert them into glucose, a molecule that releases energy when it is broken apart. Carbohydrates that are not immediately used by cells are stored in the body as glycogen and later converted into glucose as the body's activity levels require. If soccer athletes do not eat enough carbohydrates to create glycogen reserves in the body before a game, they will run out of glucose before the end of the match, and their starved muscles will perform poorly. "In soccer, muscles get the energy to work mainly from glycogen," says nutrition and sports medicine specialist Enrico Arcelli. "Players who [have] little glycogen in their muscles usually [run] less than the others."[26] Even the brain needs glucose for energy to carry out essential soccer tasks like decision making and maintaining coordination and reflexes, so a player with a poor diet may also have a poor mental performance on the field.

Some people mistakenly believe that athletes require protein more than any other nutrient, but carbohydrates in the form of foods like rice, pasta, and

A POPULAR PASTIME

200 million

Approximate number of people in the world who play soccer recreationally or competitively.

Professional soccer player Jaime Moreno takes a water break during practice. Proper hydration is critical to keeping the body ready to play at its best.

fresh vegetables are the mainstay of an athlete's diet. Carbohydrates, not protein, are the primary form of energy used by all parts of the body, from the muscles to the brain. Most soccer players eat carbohydrate-dense meals, such as a plate of rice or pasta with vegetables, about three hours before every game or practice. This way, their bodies have time to digest the carbohydrates and store glucose as glycogen to use as fuel reserves during intense physical activity.

Soccer players also must drink a lot of water to stay hydrated if they expect to perform at their full potential during a practice or a game. Having adequate water in the body helps lubricate the joints so they do not stiffen during a game. It also helps muscles contract quickly so that every time a soccer player wants to kick the ball, the muscles respond. Water helps bring oxygen to the muscles, too, and flushes out some of the lactic acid produced when muscles work anaerobically. Water also helps keep the brain working even when the rest of the body is fatigued. A well-hydrated player feels less tired during a game, pays better attention, and is less likely to feel sore the following day. The physical effects of dehydration, or lack of sufficient water in the body, can be devastating. "The loss of considerable quantities of water and salts in the form of perspiration can seriously affect athletic efficiency, causes cramps and sometimes can even damage the efficiency of our brain," says Arcelli. "The first 45 minutes [of a soccer game] can be enough to lead to a considerable dehydration rate. . . . For this reason, players should try to replenish most of the lost substances."[27] Soccer players drink water throughout the day so that they are well hydrated long before they begin to exercise and sweat heavily. It is also important for them to drink throughout a practice or a game. Athletic conditioning, muscle strength, and practice of skills cannot benefit a soccer player if the body lacks essential fuel and fluids.

Stretching It Out

A well-fed, well-hydrated soccer player builds muscle more efficiently and has greater endurance than one who is dehydrated or undernourished, and this lowers the risk of getting sore or injured during a practice or a game. But even the fittest and best-nourished soccer players may develop stiff muscles if they focus only on strength and endurance training and ignore flexibility, or the ability of muscle tissue to stretch for a greater range of motion. This is a key component of physical fitness and one that good soccer players spend time developing. "Flexibility is a basic need for the soccer athlete," say Schmid and Alejo. "An inflexible lower body makes it difficult to run at top speed, strike the ball properly, or get good height in the air while jumping."[28]

STRETCHING TO PREVENT INJURY

One of the most important ways that soccer players can avoid injury is by properly stretching before each game. These are just a few of the many stretches performed by players to help warm up key muscle groups. The red arrow points to the muscle being stretched.

1 Standing Calf Stretch

2 Butterfly Stretch (inner thigh)

4 Standing Quadriceps Stretch

3 Hamstring Stretch

All skeletal muscles work by stretching and contracting, and like a rubber band, the more often they are stretched, the more pliable they become. Muscles that are not stretched regularly may remain constantly flexed. Since muscles create all their power by flexing or contracting to move a bone, a muscle that is already contracted cannot flex any more to help swing a leg in a kick, for example. This phenomenon is called "muscle bound," and it weakens a muscle, even if it is large and well developed from strength training.

Stretching exercises improve muscle flexibility, enhancing a muscle's ability to contract. Flexibility is one of the most important aspects of training for soccer players. Not only does it improve their playing, but it is also critical for preventing sports injuries, something about which soccer players must always be wary. No matter how hard soccer players practice coordination and reflexes or how physically fit they become, an injury could bring a talented player's career to an end.

CHAPTER 5

Sidelined: Common Soccer Injuries

O
n February 23, 2008, Croatia's national soccer team, Arsenal, faced the British team, Birmingham City. One of Arsenal's top scorers, Eduardo da Silva, had the ball when Birmingham City defender Martin Taylor slid in for a tackle, a move soccer players use to knock the ball away from an opponent. Taylor's foot collided with da Silva's left shin during the play, breaking da Silva's fibula bone and badly dislocating his ankle. The game was stopped for eight minutes while da Silva was treated on the field. He was given morphine for pain before being carried away on a stretcher. The injury is one of the worst in recent soccer history, reportedly shocking even the medical staff at the playing field. According to Arsenal coach Arsène Wegner, "I've seen some bad ones before but you are not always punished with a broken leg."[29] The game ended in a tie, but da Silva's season ended on the spot.

Less than a year after his terrible injury, da Silva returned to his team. Not all injured soccer players are so lucky. Soccer is considered a sport with a medium risk of injury to players, compared to sports like American football, where the risk of injury is high. Nevertheless, soccer is a very physical game and players do get hurt, sometimes seriously. "Soccer is undoubtedly one of the most aggressive of today's sports," say sports science specialists Benny Peiser and John Minten. "Being able to be tough and play violently has become part of gaining respect."[30] Such violent play can lead to acute soccer injuries, those that occur suddenly during a game or practice. Physical training and practice help condition players' bodies to prevent acute injuries, but accidents happen. Some of the most common soccer injuries include dislocated or sprained joints, bruised and broken bones, pulled or torn muscles, and head trauma. Any of these sports-related injuries has the potential to affect a player's game, season, or entire future in the sport.

Sprains and Dislocations

When da Silva suffered a dislocated ankle, he damaged one of the most common sites of trauma for soccer athletes. Players perform many sprints and sudden turns and have frequent contact with the feet and legs of other players, all of which can put unnatural force on the ankles. The ankle joint consists of four bones—the tibia and fibula, the long bones that form the shin; the talus, a small bone that creates a ball-and-socket joint by fitting into the socket where the bases of the fibula and tibia meet; and the calcaneus, or heel bone, which supports the talus. All four bones are held together by ligaments—tough, elastic-like bands that attach bones to each other at joints. There are four major ligaments in the ankle, three on the lateral side, facing away from the opposite ankle, and one on the medial side, facing the opposite ankle. The ankle is a strong joint, designed to hold up throughout a lifetime of walking, running, and jumping, but it is not immune to severe damage, such as the major twisting that can happen during a soccer game.

If the ankle twists hard enough, the ligaments will stretch beyond their natural range of motion and may tear, either slightly or completely. Damage caused by the wrenching of ligaments is called a sprain, a serious injury that can take weeks or months to heal. Sometimes, the wrenching or twisting motion is powerful enough to dislocate a joint, or pull the ball portion of one bone out of the socket portion of another. Because ankles are such sturdy joints, a dislocated

ANATOMY OF THE ANKLE AND KNEE

In soccer, two of the most commonly injured areas are the ankle and the knee. Both areas contain numerous bones, ligaments, and tendons that can affect movement if damaged.

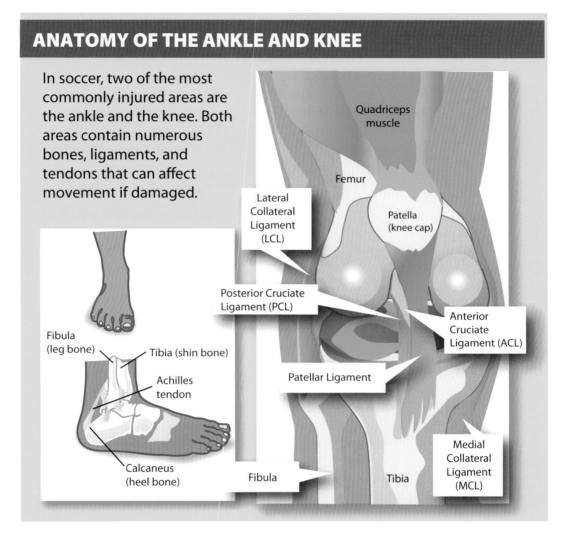

Quadriceps muscle

Femur

Lateral Collateral Ligament (LCL)

Patella (knee cap)

Posterior Cruciate Ligament (PCL)

Anterior Cruciate Ligament (ACL)

Patellar Ligament

Fibula (leg bone)

Tibia (shin bone)

Achilles tendon

Medial Collateral Ligament (MCL)

Calcaneus (heel bone)

Fibula

Tibia

ankle rarely happens unless an impact or collision breaks a shinbone. This is what happened to da Silva—his fibula was broken, making room for the talus to slide out of its socket. A dislocated joint usually causes ligament damage and can cut off the blood supply to the affected area. Dislocations are serious injuries that require emergency medical treatment.

Ankles are not the only joints that can be sprained or dislocated. Knees are another common site of injury in soccer players. The knee is a hinge joint, one that moves only back and forth. It connects the femur bone of the thigh to the tibia, the thicker of the shin's two parallel bones. The patella, a small bone often called the kneecap, is part of this joint as well. There is a pad of cartilage between the femur and the tibia called the meniscus, which acts as a cushion between the leg bones.

Several important ligaments connect the parts of the knee. The collateral ligaments run along the inner and outer sides of the joint and prevent the tibia from swinging side to side instead of front to back. Two cruciate ligaments, so named because they cross each other to form an X (*cruciate* means cross shaped), prevent the knee joint from rotating or twisting too much. One of these ligaments, the anterior cruciate ligament (ACL), keeps the knee from hyperextending, or moving beyond its natural range of motion. The other, the posterior cruciate ligament (PCL), keeps the tibia from moving too far backward.

Sprained or torn knee ligaments happen often in soccer. A tear to the ACL happens when the knee is forced to twist unnaturally. This is one of the most common and serious soccer injuries. An ACL can be torn if a sprinting player suddenly stops running to change direction, for example, or if a player's lower leg is held down by another player during an attempted turn. A torn ligament such as the ACL usually requires surgery and months of physical therapy—an exercise program that gradually adds stress and strain to an injured body part to rebuild mobility and strength. Many soccer players return to the game once a torn ligament is healed, but previously damaged joints tend to be weaker, more painful, and prone to repeat injuries. "Because of the unusual stresses placed on knees in soccer," says physician Richard Witzig, "serious knee injuries are the most common physical injury to force retirement. Indeed, more than 30% of former players will experience chronic pain."[31]

FOUL PLAY

261

Number of fouls committed during the 2010 World Cup Tournament, down from 346 committed at the 2006 World Cup.

Pulls and Tears

Unlike ligaments, which cannot be strengthened to handle more stress, muscles can be made stronger. Soccer

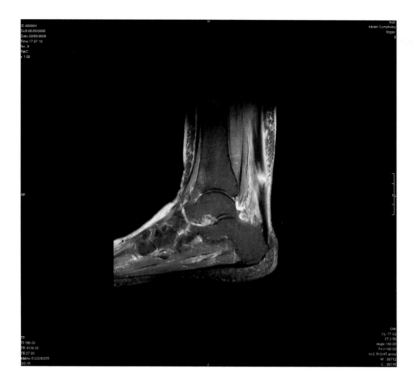

A magnetic resonance imaging (MRI) scan shows a ruptured Achilles tendon, which connects the calf muscle to the heel bone.

players' muscles are usually well adapted for playing the sport, but the muscles themselves can be sites of serious injury. They are especially vulnerable as a player begins to get tired. Overexertion, or doing more physical activity than the body can handle, sometimes results in muscle damage. So can colliding with another player. Such situations can tear a muscle's fibrous tissue. In soccer, the most common site for muscle tears, sometimes referred to as pulled muscles, are the hamstrings, a group of three muscles that run along the back of the thigh. The extent of muscle damage varies, but a torn muscle is a serious injury.

There are three levels of muscle tears. A first-degree tear involves less than 5 percent of the muscle but causes pain and stiffness. Needing a week or so to heal, a first-degree muscle tear usually causes no more problems, but if the player does not rest the muscle, the pain often does not get better. A second-degree muscle tear involves breakage across much of the muscle's tissue but stops short of tearing the muscle completely in two. A player who suffers a second-degree

WOUNDED WOMEN

Female players are more than twice as likely as males to damage their anterior cruciate ligament (ACL) while playing soccer.

tear usually cannot contract the muscle at all without severe pain. This kind of tear often can be felt through the skin as a bump or a dent in the muscle. A third-degree muscle tear is a rupture, a complete tear that separates the muscle in two. The muscle is then completely unable to contract, and the player cannot move the affected limb normally. The torn ends of the ruptured muscle may ball up to form large lumps under the skin. This injury also causes internal bleeding at the site of the rupture. Ruptured muscles require surgery to join the pieces of muscle back together. Even after the muscle heals, scar tissue remains. This weakens and stiffens the muscle and makes it vulnerable to future injuries.

Just as muscles cannot work properly when badly torn, a muscle will be useless if its tendon, the band of fibrous tissue that connects it to a bone, is damaged. One of the most important tendons for soccer athletes is the Achilles tendon, which connects the muscle of the calf to the calcaneus (heel bone). The Achilles tendon is essential for walking, running, and jumping, but the force put on this tendon during an aggressive soccer game is sometimes too much. If the tendon tears, either partly or completely, then the calf muscle will be unable to contract normally. Without its anchor to the heel, the muscle may ball up in the back of the leg. The player will be unable to run or even walk.

An injured Achilles tendon usually requires surgery and can have serious consequences for soccer players. English soccer phenomenon David Beckham, one of the world's best-known players, suffered a torn Achilles tendon in March 2010. Needing six months to properly recover, the thirty-four-year-old missed the 2010 World Cup that summer. He would have been the first English player to compete in four World Cup tournaments. "He felt the muscle begin to come up, which is a typical symptom when you break an Achilles' tendon," Beckham's coach, Leonardo Araujo, told reporters. "This is a real blow."[32]

A Bad Break

Serious bone injuries can end a player's season or even career. In October 2004, Djibril Cisse, an offensive striker for France's professional-league team, suffered a severe compound fracture of his left tibia and fibula; both bones had snapped in half. The break was so bad that his doctors were unsure how much time he would need to recover or if he would ever return to professional soccer. Although he missed the rest of the season, Cisse did recuperate in time to return to his team the following year and regain his status as a top scorer. But in 2006, shortly before the World Cup, Cisse suffered another fracture, this time to his right tibia, and it cost him his spot on France's World Cup team.

After years of recovery and hard work to get back in shape, Cisse finally made it to the World Cup in 2010, again playing for France. But his long journey to get there shows the many challenges a broken bone can place on a soccer player. Some who suffer this debilitating injury never play professionally again.

Bruised and Broken Bones

Injuries to ligaments, muscles, and tendons can have major consequences for soccer players, but the bones to which the muscles, ligaments, and tendons attach, especially in the lower leg, are also put into many risky situations during a game. High-speed, high-force kicks and tackles in soccer often pit one player's feet and shins against another's, causing a clash of bones. Bones are strong, but they can be damaged by a forceful blow, such as a high-speed collision between soccer players. A crack or break in a bone's surface is called a fracture.

Bones consist of a dense outer covering called compact bone, which surrounds a core of blood-rich spongy bone (also called bone marrow). A fracture in a bone's surface is a serious injury that usually causes severe pain and swelling in the tissues surrounding the bone. Most bone fractures

require medical treatment, which includes repositioning the broken bone and encasing the limb in a cast for several weeks to give the bone tissue time to heal. Some bone fractures are worse than others. The best-case scenario for a broken bone is a closed or simple fracture—a crack in the bone that does not cause part of the bone to shift and damage surrounding tissue. A worse kind of break is a compound or open fracture, in which the bone on either side of the fracture spears into surrounding tissue or even pierces through the skin. Compound fractures can cause serious bleeding and tissue damage as well as excruciating pain. They require surgery and the use of plates, screws, and wires to realign the bones properly. A third type of fracture is a comminuted fracture, one in which the bone tissue shatters into pieces. This kind of fracture may also require surgery and a long period of recovery during which the bone must be kept immobile in a cast in order to heal.

In soccer, a bone may be hit forcefully but not quite hard enough to fracture it. The bone may become bruised if blood vessels in the spongy bone are ruptured and leak into the

Becoming a Physical Therapist

Physical therapists are health-care professionals who develop individualized plans of treatment for patients who cannot move and function normally because of an injury or other medical condition. Physical therapists help athletes recover after a severe injury, such as a broken bone or a torn muscle, ligament, or tendon. They create a plan for each patient to reduce pain, restore range of motion, and keep muscles strong and flexible while the patient is recovering. Physical therapists help injured athletes return to competition as quickly as possible. They need a master's or doctorate degree in physical therapy and must pass their state's required examinations in order to obtain a license to practice. They are employed by hospitals, clinics, or private practices and often work evenings and weekends to fit their patients' schedules. They require good interpersonal skills and empathy when working with athletes, who often need special encouragement and may fear their career in their sport is over if their injury was severe. Physical therapists earn an average of fifty thousand dollars to more than a hundred thousand dollars a year. The job market for physical therapists is strong and is expected to grow.

A young athlete works out under the supervision of a physical therapist, who is trained to create an exercise plan and monitor progress to improve strength and ensure recovery from injuries.

surrounding tissue. Bruised bones can be as painful as bone fractures and cause a similar amount of swelling. A bruise is often the diagnoses when an X-ray of the injury does not show a fracture in the bone. Most bone bruises heal within days. Although painful, they rarely cause a player to miss out on the remainder of a season the way bone fractures can.

On the soccer field, serious bone injuries are uncommon among young players. As players get older, however, the risk of bone trauma is greater. In college-level and professional leagues, where soccer players move fast and are very physical and competitive, bone injuries are more common. Because severely broken bones are some of the most shocking and memorable injuries that occur on a soccer field, they receive a lot of attention from spectators, coaches, referees, and players. After a particularly bad incident, such as da Silva's leg and ankle injuries, the player who caused a collision is sometimes accused of foul play. But in a game as fast paced as soccer, players know that collisions hard enough to break bones are bound to happen. "You don't have time to think!" says Andy Townsend, a former World Cup soccer player with the Republic of Ireland. "The ball breaks, you have to go and win it. That's your job."[33]

Facing Injuries Head On

Most soccer injuries happen below the waist, but the head can also be at risk. Soccer is a unique sport in that players wear no helmets or protective headgear, yet they frequently strike their heads against the ball to stop its progress, move it up the field, or try to score a goal. Soccer players head the ball an average of six to eight times in every game. Some sports medicine experts suspect that repeatedly heading the ball might cause many small head injuries that accumulate to cause brain damage in some players, much the way professional boxers sometimes suffer brain damage from taking repeated blows to the head and face.

An even bigger concern in soccer, however, is a single, hard blow to the head that causes a concussion, an injury that happens when the brain slams against the inside of the skull. Only 2 to 3 percent of soccer injuries are concussions, but they are among the most serious. Severe concussions in soccer are more often a result of hitting another player, a goal post, or the ground than heading the ball. Sometimes, soccer players dive or fall to the ground, and their head is suddenly on the same level as other players' kicking feet. Goalkeepers often find themselves in such a position as they lunge for the ball to keep the other team from scoring. A hard kick to the face or the head can be life threatening. Even more than a broken bone or a tear to a muscle, tendon, or ligament, a head injury can remove a player from the game of soccer

permanently. "Sports concussions are in fact far more serious than most people realize," says the Institute of Medicine (IOM). "A concussion releases a cascade of reactions in the brain that can last for weeks, and make it particularly vulnerable to damage from an additional concussion." Many athletes, says the IOM, "have been forced to abandon their sports and their career aspirations because they never fully recovered from concussions."[34]

A player from the Spanish national team takes a kick to the head during a 2010 World Cup game. Injuries to the head can be particularly serious or life-threatening.

Suiting Up for Safety

Despite the risks soccer poses to the head and the rest of the body, players equip themselves with very little protective gear. Compared to sports such as American football and hockey, in which nearly every inch of a player's body is helmeted or padded, a soccer player's only protection comes from thin pads called shin guards worn over the shins and ankles to minimize pain and injury caused by getting kicked

Shin guards, worn under the socks, are the only piece of protective equipment that soccer players wear.

in these sensitive spots. A soccer player's one piece of armor seems to offer little protection. About 90 percent of injuries caused by force to the lower legs happen when the players are wearing shin guards. Although the risk of serious injury in soccer is less than in sports like American football, many competitive soccer players have seen a fellow player get hurt or have suffered some kind of injury themselves. Knowing that serious injuries are possible and that the equipment to protect them from injuries is almost nonexistent, soccer players have to train themselves to step onto the field without fear. The ability to do so takes a strong frame of mind, something experts say needs to be trained and conditioned just as much as the physical body. Success at the game of soccer depends as much on psychology as the physical ability of the body to keep up with the game.

CHAPTER **6**

Think Fast: The Psychology of Soccer

The numerous injuries that can be suffered in soccer are proof that it is a very physical sport. In order to play their best and avoid getting hurt, soccer players put a great deal of time and energy into conditioning their bodies for the rigors of the sport. However, a soccer match consists of more than physical ability. The best players exhibit not only athletic ability but also intelligence. Some players seem to have a sixth sense for anticipating what is going to happen next and acting before it does. Last-second shots on goal, heart-stopping saves, and unforeseen interceptions delight crowds and often surprise even the players on the field. Soccer moves fast, and the outcome of every game is unpredictable. Even the best teams have "off" days, and underdogs can and often do win matches. This is one of the reasons soccer is so wildly popular with fans around the world—its swiftness and unpredictability make it exciting and suspenseful.

The fast pace of a soccer game demands some fast thinking from players. The use of reflexes—automatic physical responses to what the senses perceive—is one way a soccer athlete's brain works on the field, but soccer also requires actual thinking, not just good reflexes. Great soccer playing is a mental as much as a physical activity. Victory is often based on how intelligently individuals and teams play a game. Success also depends on how well players and teams cope emotionally with the failures that happen during the match, things like missed passes and other mistakes. Teams can lose their confidence during a game if their attention slips and the other team takes the lead. Players must learn to tune out stress and stay focused, because the brain's thinking power, more than any physical trait, makes the difference between a good player and a star, a decent team and an unstoppable one. "The psychological part of the game is one of those intangibles that cannot be measured, but it's every bit as important as the rest, if not more so,"[35] says retired college soccer coach Michael Parker. Without psychology, the science of human mental processes and behavior, soccer would not be the world phenomenon that it is today.

Becoming a Sports Psychologist

Sports psychologists are professionals who help athletes cope with the psychological and emotional stresses that can affect how they play their sport. A sports psychologist may counsel athletes about problems in their personal lives, for example, or work with them on developing healthy attitudes toward games and matches by visualizing themselves playing well. Since stress can be a significant problem for athletes, sports psychology is a growing field. Those interested in this career require at least a master's degree in psychology, paired with education and/or experience in sports science and working with athletes. Sports psychologists may work for a professional sports team; for a high school, college, or university; or in private practice. They often travel, especially if they work with professional athletes. The salary for this job ranges from forty-five thousand to eighty thousand dollars per year or more.

The Art of Faking

Soccer players keep themselves in good physical condition, but the ability to run fast, jump high, and kick powerfully account for only part of what happens during a soccer game. These physical abilities are tools that help a player carry out great plays, but the plays themselves originate in the player's mind as he or she makes split-second decisions about how to intercept a ball or where to pass it. Soccer is not a contest for who can kick the ball the hardest. It is a contest of who is the smartest and sneakiest. Players try to trick opponents into thinking they are going to do one thing or move one way; then they do something else. On offense, the trickiest players are the most likely to score goals. On defense, the

Chris Rolfe, right, uses a backwards kick to keep the ball away from Landon Donovan, left, in a 2006 match between the Chicago Fire and the Los Angeles Galaxy. Such a move is known as a feint, a tactic soccer players often use to fool their opponents.

A FAMOUS FIRST

Spain won the 2010 World Cup after losing to Switzerland in its first tournament game. No other team has ever bounced back to win a World Cup title after losing its first match.

players least likely to fall for the offense's tricks are the most successful at defending their goal. At times, soccer is like a complex game of keep-away. Players are thinking, planning, and analyzing constantly.

One psychological trick soccer players master is the feint. A feint, or fake, is designed to fool the eyes of players who are trying to take away the ball. Since soccer players cannot use their hands, they use small kicks called dribbles to keep the ball in front of them while running. As a player dribbles, opponents run up and try to steal the ball away. When adversaries close in and pressure the player with the ball, that player may feint to try to get around the opposition. "A typical patterned movement or feint to escape pressure is to play the ball behind the standing leg," explain college soccer coaches James W. Lennox, Janet Rayfield, and Bill Steffen. "Facing an opponent, the player steps beyond the ball with one leg and then pulls the ball behind the standing leg with the inside of the other foot."[36] Another type of feint is a step over, when the player who is dribbling the ball actually steps over it instead of tapping it like the opponent expects, then quickly kicks it in a different direction—hopefully before the opponent can react.

Successful feints allow players to keep the ball away from opponents so they can pass it to a teammate or shoot it at the goal. Good players are masters of such trickery. The Brazilian soccer legend Pelé was so good at feinting that he could even pull off tricks like the sombrero (Spanish for hat), in which he would pop the ball up into the air and over his opponent's head only to dash around him and reclaim the ball as it came down. Such moves left Pelé's opponents gaping in wonder and his fans cheering wildly from the stands.

Pelé was such a quick thinker that no one ever quite knew what to expect from him on the field. Most players, however, rely on just a few kinds of feints that they have perfected. Offensive players, in particular, tend to be excellent fakers, since they have to get around the defenders standing between them and the goal. Defenders have their own special talents, though. They have seen most feints enough times to get good at reading a player's body movements and predicting what kind of trick is about to be tried. Good defenders are masters at the art of anticipation—predicting what other players will do and acting before they do it. "The player is able to put himself in the position of his opponent in order to find out what he would do in the same situation," says worldwide coaching expert Horst Wein. "When an intelligent defender looks at the passes from the [offensive player's] point of view he is able to lift his defensive game to a much higher level."[37] Players learn to anticipate things like the flight direction, speed, height, and spin of the ball based on the kicking player's position and movements. They also determine, from players' body language, when a pass or a challenge is likely to happen. Often, they can even predict what kind of move a particular player will use in a given situation. Anticipation is one of the things that make good soccer players appear as if they have a sixth sense on the field.

It All Comes Down to Teamwork

It is crucial to be able to predict what opponents are about to do in a game, but soccer players must also anticipate what their own teammates are going to do. Soccer is a sport in which individual players often have moments of excellence, but the best players are those who see themselves as a piece of the whole. "The player should never seek to shine on a personal level," says Wein, "but instead try to play his role as part of an effective team."[38] Even Pelé knew that it was often better to pass the ball to a teammate than try to score himself, and many of his most memorable plays were assists—he would make a brilliant pass to a teammate, who was then the one to score. The best soccer teams work together easily, each player knowing the others so well that they anticipate each other's next moves and pass the ball back and forth with ease. "Good soccer teams are looked

A soccer coach gives instruction to his team. Good coaching and teamwork are critical to success on the field.

upon as a complete unit, meshing everybody's roles and responsibilities,"[39] says Parker.

The coach has a critical role in developing team unity. In some sports, like American football, the coaches control nearly everything the team does in the game, deciding from the sidelines which plays the team should use next and communicating this to the players through hand gestures. In soccer, coaches stay on the sidelines during the game and have little opportunity to tell their team what to do next. "Even if, nowadays, the coach is allowed to give players tactical advice during the match, there will be many situations where oral instruction is impossible,"[40] say professional soccer coaches Jens Bangsbo and Birger Pietersen. Soccer coaches are responsible for teaching their players how to focus on each other and make their own decisions during a game, not look to the sidelines for directions from the coach. A critical part of soccer coaching is training players to think for themselves. The team's success or failure on the field largely depends on the development of their ability to read the movements and intentions of the opposing team and their own teammates. Learning to predict the actions of fellow players leads to successful plays and victorious games. It also builds team confidence, a critical psychological element for success in soccer.

When Momentum Shifts

Team confidence is closely linked to what spectators, players, coaches, and announcers call the momentum of a game. Momentum, literally meaning movement, generally refers

A goalkeeper watches the ball fly past her into the net. An unexpected goal can be a turning point in a game, shifting momentum from one team to another.

LOW SCORES

145

Number of goals scored at the 2010 World Cup in South Africa, the lowest total since the tournament changed to a sixty-four-game format in 1998.

to how players interact with their teammates and their opponents to move the ball. It is measured in part by how much time the ball spends on each half of the field—a team that is constantly on the defensive, trying to keep the ball away from its own goal, is usually the team that lacks momentum in a game, while momentum usually belongs to the team that keeps the ball near its opponents' goal much of the time. Momentum also involves how well players anticipate each other's movements and how confident they feel. In soccer, the losing team is usually the one with the least confidence, but confidence levels can change in a match. Because the final score in soccer matches is usually low and teams often win by as little as a single goal, the victor in many games is not known until the full ninety minutes are up. A last-minute, game-saving goal is often possible, and a losing team can pull together and bounce back from what seems like certain defeat. When this happens, the momentum of the entire game may shift. The team that was winning may lose focus and confidence, while the team that was losing may rebound and take over the momentum of the game.

Unexpected goals are one example of a turning point, a moment in a soccer game in which one team's confidence surges while the other team loses its competitive edge. "It is often a double-change in the mentality of both teams, revolving around an incident or series of incidents in a match, that creates the biggest changes in momentum," says Alistair Higham, an expert lecturer on momentum in sports. "In effect, the change in mentality brings about a change in performance."[41] Goals are not the only kind of turning point in a soccer game. A fabulous save by a goalkeeper or defensive player, loss of a key player due to injury, or a referee's decision are other examples of things that can shift momentum in a game. "It may be as simple as one of your players, for want of a better word, destroying someone who has the ball at his feet with a magnificent tackle," says Dick Bate, elite coaching manager of the English Football Association. "The tackle can arouse a team to become inspired because of his one act. And it can be as simple as that."[42] Momentum shifts also can be created by the crowd watching the game. The energy of spectators, either positive or negative, can boost the spirits of one team and cause the other team to falter. Soccer games are, after all, public performances. The pressure of feeling like one is on stage during a game and how well a player deals with that pressure is where soccer psychology sometimes matters most.

A Stressful Situation

Stress in soccer comes from a variety of sources. High expectations from coaches and teammates can lead to fear of disappointing them if a player makes a mistake. Players

A dejected David Beckham, kneeling, is taunted by Alpay Ozalan after missing a penalty kick during a match between England and Turkey in 2003. After the game, Beckham endured harsh criticism from both the press and fans.

may also dread facing a very physical, brutal team. They may fear suffering a terrible injury during a match, especially if they have seen a teammate get horribly injured or if they already have pain and tenderness from a previous injury. The most significant source of stress for soccer players, however, can be the crowd. Players often feel enormous pressure to perform heroically or risk disappointing their fans with a loss. Soccer is deeply linked to the culture of many communities and even entire countries. A high school or college soccer match against the school's chief rival, for example, places tremendous pressure on players to win, since fans (who are also the players' peers) often respond to a loss with disappointment, anger, and even violence. At the professional level, the crowds are much bigger and the stakes are even higher. Every four years at the World Cup tournament, where each team represents an entire nation, players may feel that their country's world reputation is on the line. A mistake or a missed opportunity not only will be witnessed by thousands of spectators in the stands but will also be replayed, analyzed, and criticized on television and in the news, possibly for years to come. Fear of public humiliation is a powerful factor in a soccer athlete's performance. Ironically, the better the player is, the worse the pressure may be, since crowds expect perfection from their team's stars. Such a player may perceive that mistakes will be unforgivable, and the pressure to perform flawlessly can be overwhelming.

Especially at the professional level, months and years of physical training and practice mean nothing if players cannot hold up emotionally under pressure. How well each player is able to deal with the tremendous stress of a public soccer performance can determine the outcome of a match. Regardless of how physically talented a player is, psychological strength is the true heart of soccer. "Players think, feel, and then act, in that order," says Bill Beswick, who has been the team psychologist for England's national soccer teams since 1995. "Soccer challenges the player's thoughts and feelings, and often success is doing what it takes in spite of their fears."[43] Players who succeed at high levels of the game do so because they find a way to cope with their own

How Beckham Bends It

British-born soccer phenomenon David Beckham is one of the most-recognized sports stars in the world. He was born May 2, 1975, and joined England's professional soccer team when he was just seventeen years old. He has played in three World Cup tournaments and twice has been named World Player of the Year in soccer. Beckham is famous for his legendary free kicks. The gifted midfielder can kick a soccer ball on a path that curves at the last second to land in the corner of the net. His "ball bending" skills look like magic, but Beckham actually uses aerodynamics to bend a ball's path through the air. When he kicks a ball slightly off center, it spins during its flight. The spin pulls a pocket of air around the ball, and this reduces the air pressure on one side of the ball compared to the other, so the ball's flight path curves. The explanation for Beckham's jaw-dropping goals may be scientific, but many of his fans see something celestial in it. According to a 2004 survey conducted by the British Broadcasting Corporation, 37 percent of the British population believed David Beckham had godlike powers.

Superstar David Beckham prepares for a kick during a game with the Los Angeles Galaxy in 2007. He is known for his ability to "bend" the ball, sending it on a curved path through the air.

stress and fear and play the game in spite of these potentially crippling forces.

Perhaps the most stressful position on the soccer field belongs to the player charged with protecting the goal, since every point scored ultimately comes down to a ball that slips past the goalkeeper and into the net. "The pressures on goalkeepers are enormous," says Parker. "A mistake in this position is more amplified than in any other, often making her a hero or a goat [failure]. It takes a special type of personality to play this position."[44] All eyes are on the goalkeeper when a team gets close to scoring. This is never more true than during a penalty kick, which is awarded if the referee determines that one team has broken a rule. That team is then penalized by giving a player on the other team an opportunity to kick the ball unchallenged. Players from the other team may be allowed to stand in front of the goal to form a wall, but the goalkeeper is the main player responsible for preventing a score. A penalty kick may determine who wins or loses a soccer match, so the pressure on the goalkeeper to catch or deflect the ball in this situation is extreme, and the pressure on the kicker can be equally intense. One of the most famous failed penalty kicks in soccer history occurred when England's David Beckham, notorious for his kicking accuracy, slipped and missed a crucial penalty shot in a 2003 tournament game against Turkey. Fans and the English press were quick to turn on Beckham, who had been widely touted as a national hero in England. "A player of his profile and reputation needed to offer England so much more than he did here,"[45] writes BBC sports reporter Phil McNulty in an article titled "What Went Wrong with Beckham?" Such articles show how much pressure public expectations can put on soccer players to perform flawlessly on the field and the criticism that will punish them if they fail.

Only Human

Like countless other cases of soccer heroes who disappoint their fans and suffer public humiliation because of it, Beckham seemed to face an ongoing psychological battle with the game once he had a few tastes of defeat. Perhaps because soccer demands such outstanding physical conditioning, technical skill, and a sixth-sense style of play from those who undertake it, fans may come to think of great soccer players as superhuman. But even players with infamous strength, endurance, talent, and skill are not immune to injuries, exhaustion, and the power of negative thinking on the field. Soccer brings out the best qualities in its best players, but it can also show human limitations at their worst. Yet players continue to come to the field, and billions of soccer fans the world over continue to love the game with a passion unrivaled by any other sport on Earth. Soccer blends all parts of science—physical, biological, and psychological—into a complex pastime that only becomes more popular with time. Soccer is truly a sport for the people, and as Pelé called it, the ultimate beautiful game.

NOTES

Chapter 1: The People's Game

1. Quoted in David Goldblatt. *The Ball Is Round: A Global History of Soccer*. New York: Riverhead, 2006, p. 3.
2. Nigel B. Crowther. *Sport in Ancient Times*. Westport, CT: Praeger, 2007, p. 4.
3. Goldblatt. *The Ball Is Round*. p. 12.
4. Richard Witzig. *The Global Art of Soccer*. New Orleans, LA: Cusiboy, 2006, p. 9.
5. Quoted in Jean Fievet. "Will World Cup 2010 Be Most-Watched TV Event?" ABC News International, June 11, 2010, http://abcnews .go.com/International/Media/ world-cup-mania-kicks-off-world/ story?id=10884963.
6. Witzig. *Global Art of Soccer*. p. 7.

Chapter 2: Goal Setting: The Physics of a Soccer Match

7. John Wesson. *The Science of Soccer*. New York: Taylor & Francis, 2002, p. 72.
8. Seyed Hamid Hamraz and Seyed Shams Feyzabadi. "General Purpose Learning Machine Using K-Nearest Neighbors Algorithm." In *Robot Soccer World Cup IX*, edited by Ansgar Bredenfeld, Adam Jacoff, Itsuki Noda, and Yasutake Takahashi. Berlin, Germany: Springer-Verlag, 2006, p. 532.
9. Wesson. *Science of Soccer*. p. 81.
10. Jim Puhalla, Jeff Krans, and Mike Goatley. *Sports Fields: A Manual for Design Construction and Maintenance*. Hoboken, NJ: John Wiley & Sons, 1999, p. 278.
11. Puhalla, Krans, and Goatley. *Sports Fields*. p. 278.
12. Quoted in FIFA.com. "FIFA Quality Concept for Footballs." FIFA.com. http://footballs.fifa.com/Experts-Opinion/Ottmar-Hitzfeld.
13. Quoted in FIFA.com. "FIFA Quality Concept for Footballs." FIFA.com. http://footballs.fifa.com/Experts-Opinion/Urs-Meier.

Chapter 3: Look! No Hands! The Biomechanics of Playing Soccer

14. Pekka Luhtanen. "Biomechanical Aspects." In *Football (Soccer)*, edited by Björn Ekblom. Oxford, UK: Blackwell Scientific, 1994, p. 64.

15. Danny Mielke. *Soccer Fundamentals*. Champaign, IL: Human Kinetics, 2003, p. 31.
16. Cameron Bauer. *Algebra for Athletes*, 2nd ed. New York: Nova Science, 2007, p. 96.
17. Luhtanen. "Biomechanical Aspects." p. 67.
18. Luhtanen. "Biomechanical Aspects." p. 66.
19. Gene Klein. "Corner Kicks and Throw-Ins." In *Attacking Soccer: Tactics and Drills for High-Scoring Offense*, edited by Joseph A. Luxbacher. Champaign, IL: Human Kinetics, 1999, p. 107.
20. Peter Mellor and Tony Waiters. "Goalkeeping Excellence." In *The Soccer Coaching Bible*, edited by the National Soccer Coaches Association of America. Champaign, IL: Human Kinetics, 2004, pp. 164, 167.

Chapter 4: The Right Condition: Physical Training for Soccer Players

21. Witzig. *Global Art of Soccer*. p. 25.
22. Ron McEachen. "Training for High-Level Soccer Fitness." In *The Soccer Coaching Bible*, edited by the National Soccer Coaches Association of America. Champaign, IL: Human Kinetics, 2004, p. 116.
23. Pelé. *My Life and the Beautiful Game: The Autobiography of Soccer's Greatest Star*. New York: Doubleday, 1977, p. 88.
24. McEachen. "Training for High-Level Soccer Fitness." p. 118.
25. Sigi Schmid and Bob Alejo. *Complete Conditioning for Soccer*. Champaign, IL: Human Kinetics, 2002, p. 3.
26. Enrico Arcelli. *Nutrition for Soccer Players*. Spring City, PA: Reedswain, 1998, p. 14.
27. Arcelli. *Nutrition for Soccer Players*. pp. 12, 14.
28. Schmid and Alejo. *Complete Conditioning for Soccer*. pp. 2, 20.

Chapter 5: Sidelined: Common Soccer Injuries

29. Quoted in ESPN Soccernet. "Eduardo Suffers Horror Injury at St. Andrews." ESPN Soccernet, February 23, 2008, http://soccernet.espn.go.com/news/story?id=510495&cc=5901.
30. Benny Peiser and John Minten. "Soccer Violence." In *Science and Soccer*, 2nd ed., edited by Thomas A. Reilly and A. Mark Williams. New York: Routledge, 2003, p. 232.
31. Witzig. *Global Art of Soccer*. p. 108.
32. Quoted in *USA TODAY*. "AP: Beckham Out of World Cup After Tearing Achilles' Tendon." *USA TODAY*, March 15, 2010, http://www.usatoday.com/sports/soccer/2010-03-14-beckham-injury_N.htm.
33. Quoted in MailOnline.com. "Crunch Time: Aaron Ramsey's Broken Leg Is a Wake-Up Call for the Game of Pain." MailOnline.com, March 2, 2010, http://www.dailymail.co.uk/sport/football/article-1254694/

Crunch-time-Aaron-Ramseys-bro-ken-leg-wake-game-pain.html.

34. Institute of Medicine. *Is Soccer Bad for Children's Heads? Summary of the IOM Workshop on Neuropsychological Consequences of Head Impact in Youth Soccer.* Washington, DC: National Academy Press, 2003, p. 1.

Chapter 6: Think Fast: The Psychology of Soccer

35. Michael Parker. *Premier Soccer: Skills, Tactics, & Strategies for Winning Play.* Champaign, IL: Human Kinetics, 2008, p. 24.
36. James W. Lennox, Janet Rayfield, and Bill Steffen. *Soccer Skills & Drills.* Champaign, IL: Human Kinetics, 2006, p. 7.
37. Horst Wein. *Developing Game Intelligence in Soccer.* Spring City, PA: Reedswain, 2004, p. 297.
38. Wein. *Developing Game Intelligence in Soccer.* p. 297.
39. Parker. *Premier Soccer.* p. 16.
40. Jens Bangsbo and Birger Pietersen. *Soccer Systems & Strategies.* Champaign, IL: Human Kinetics, 2000, p. 55.
41. Alistair Higham. "The Pattern of the Match." In *Momentum in Soccer: Controlling the Game,* edited by Alistair Higham, Chris Harwood, and Andy Kale. Leeds, UK: Coachwise Ltd., 2005, p. 22.
42. Quoted in Higham. "Pattern of the Match." p. 22.
43. Bill Beswick. *Focused for Soccer: How to Win the Mental Game.* Champaign, IL: Human Kinetics, 2010, p. 6.
44. Parker. *Premier Soccer.* p. 16.
45. Phil McNulty. "What Went Wrong with Beckham?" BBC Sport, June 25, 2004, http://news.bbc.co.uk/sport2/hi/football/euro_2004/england/3839357.stm.

GLOSSARY

acute injury: An injury caused by a single, sudden event, such as an impact.

anaerobic exercise: Physical activity the body performs after the muscles have used up their stores of oxygen.

biomechanics: The scientific study of biological activity and movement.

center of gravity: The single point within the body where mass is concentrated so the body is equally balanced in all directions.

central nervous system: The parts of the brain and spinal cord that receive and process stimuli from the body and coordinate appropriate physical responses.

dehydration: A condition in which the body's fluid levels are too low.

dimensions: Mathematical measurements of the boundaries of an object or area.

endurance: The ability to tolerate difficult physical activity for a long period of time.

feint: A faked movement designed to mislead an opponent from one's intended direction or purpose.

flexibility: The ability of muscle tissue to stretch for a greater range of motion around a joint.

friction: The force that slows down movement between two objects in contact with each other.

glucose: The molecule that the cells of the body break down for energy.

glycogen: A molecule that stores extra glucose from carbohydrates until the body is ready to break the glucose down for energy.

glycolysis: The process by which glucose molecules are broken down by the cells to release energy.

lever: A bar used to apply force to an object at one end by putting pressure on the other end.

ligament: A tough, fibrous band of tissue connecting two bones together at a joint.

mass: The measurement of an object's size and how much material it contains.

perimeter: The outer boundary of a geometric figure.

physical therapy: The treatment of a disease, injury, or disability using exercises to restore or increase strength, functionality, and range of motion.

physics: The scientific study of matter and energy.

reflex: An instantaneous, automatic bodily response to a stimulus.

stimulus: An event or condition in a person's environment that is perceived by the brain and causes a physical reaction.

tendon: A tough, fibrous band of tissue that connects a muscle to a bone.

trajectory: The path of a moving object.

velocity: The relationship between the distance a moving object travels and the time it takes; speed.

FOR MORE INFORMATION

Books

Suzanne Bazemore. *Soccer: How It Works.* Mankato, MN: Capstone Press, 2010. Explains some of the scientific principles on which soccer is based. Part of the Sports Illustrated for Kids Science of Sports series.

John Eric Goff. *Gold Medal Physics: The Science of Sports.* Baltimore, MD: Johns Hopkins University Press, 2009. Analyzes famous moments in soccer and other sports from a scientific point of view.

Tom Reilly. *The Science of Training Soccer: A Scientific Approach to Developing Strength, Speed, and Endurance.* New York: Routledge, 2007. Describes how biology and biomechanics principles are used when developing a training program for soccer players.

John Wesson. *The Science of Soccer.* New York: Taylor & Francis, 2002. Discusses probability, ideal body size for players, physics of the ball and its bounce, and scientific reasons why soccer game rules were developed.

DVDs

History of Soccer: The Beautiful Game. DVD. Directed by Richard Foos. Los Angeles, CA: Shout Factory, 2003. This six-volume DVD set gives a comprehensive history of soccer, including player profiles, footage of the first moving pictures of soccer in 1897, and interviews with soccer greats.

Periodicals

Dave Munger. "Football's Confounding Physics." *Seed Magazine*, September 16, 2010, www.seedmagazine.com/content/article/footballs_counfounding_physics/. Explains how the flight of a soccer ball curves and why certain kicks can fool even an experienced goalie.

Websites

Fédération Internationale de Football Association (www.FIFA.com). Provides recaps of famous World Cup events, information about teams around the world, a history of competitive world soccer, and more.

Science of Soccer Online (www.scienceofsocceronline.com). Useful information based on cutting-edge sports science research, with information on nutrition, injuries, and psychology for soccer players.

Soccer Ball World (www.soccerball world.com). Describes soccer ball history, how modern balls are made, and new developments in soccer ball technology.

U.S. Soccer Federation (www.ussoccer .com). Features information on teams, coaches, news, and game statistics for American men's and women's soccer.

INDEX

PICTURE CREDITS

Cover: photos.com/Getty Images
Aaron Penley/Hulton Archive/Getty Images, 14
© Action Plus Sports Images/Alamy, 78
AFP/Getty Images, 38
AP Images/Denis Farrell, 61
AP Images/Dusan Vranic, 45
AP Images/Jeff Roberson, 81
AP Images/Julie Jacobson, 60
AP Images/Nam Y. Huh, 63
AP Images/Rebecca Blackwell, 43
AP Images/Shizuo Kambayashi, 58
Bob Thomas/Bob Thomas Sports Photography/Getty Images, 30
© ceredigionpix/Alamy, 74
© Daniel Kaesler/Alamy, 23
© David Crausby/Alamy, 50
Doug Pensinger/Getty Images, 77
Gale/Cengage Learning, 20, 26, 35, 41, 65, 69

Greg Wood/AFP/Getty Images, 89
Gustoimages/Photo Researchers, Inc., 71
Hulton Archive/Getty Images, 18
© Jack Carey/Alamy, 34
© James Caldwell/Alamy, 75
Jamie Squire/Getty Images, 32
© Jim West/Alamy, 84
Koichi Kamoshida/Getty Images, 9
Lars Baron/Bongarts/Getty Images, 85
Lefty Shivambu/Gallo Images/Getty Images, 39
© O'Sullivan/Alamy, 57
Popperfoto/Getty Images, 16, 17
© Robert Harding Picture Library Ltd/Alamy, 12
© Robin Russell/Alamy, 28
Ross Kinnaird/Getty Images, 87
Tony Karumba/AFP/Getty Images, 21
Warrick Page/Getty Images, 47

ABOUT THE AUTHOR

Jenny MacKay is the author of twelve nonfiction books for middle-grade and teen readers. She lives with her husband, son, and daughter in northern Nevada, where she was born and raised. In addition to writing books and tutoring college students in writing, MacKay is now a soccer mom to her six-year-old daughter, who recently took up the sport.